EA

There's a clock inside of us that contains our true intention, and when we ignore its ticking we do so at our own peril.

Herbert Holt, M.D.
Free To Be Good Or Bad

SO WHAT MAKES YOU TICK?

David Sharpe

Ten Speed Press
Berkeley, California

1🟊

TEN SPEED PRESS
P.O. Box 7123
Berkeley, California 94707

Library of Congress Cataloging-in-Publication Date
Sharpe, David, 1951-
So, what makes you tick? /David Sharpe.
p. cm.
ISBN 0-89815-372-7
1. Celebrities–United States–Correspondence. 2. Conduct of life. I. Title.
CT220.S49 1990
920.073–dc20
90-38626
CIP

Text design by Barry Mitchell
Cover design by Fifth Street Design
Cover art by Barry Mitchell
Typesetting by Communication Arts, Inc.

An Atticus Press Book

Printed in the United States of America

First Edition

1   2   3   4   5   —   94   93   92   91   90

To my Mother and Father

and

Ernest, my brother

THE CLOCK OF THE YEARS

Every man
is his own clock
               Tic toc
he may rise
by the sun
and go to sleep
with the stars
               Tic toc
but if he
take stock
and come to knock
at fate's door
he may find
that he himself
has sprung the lock
against himself.
Useless
to knock
now, the door
will not open—
save only
at the shock
of love,
to deliver him
from that block,
unlock
his heart and
set it beating again:
               Tic toc
               Tic toc
               Tic toc!

                    William Carlos Williams

CONTENTS

TO EXPRESS THE UNIVERSE DEPOSITED WITHIN US

I WANT TO KNOW THE TRUTH ABOUT EVERYTHING

CONTENTS

I AM BUT THE SMALLEST OF COGS, PART OF AN IMMENSE UNIVERSAL CLOCK

THE FUN OF LIVING IS MYSTERY

CONTENTS

ONE THOUSAND HOURS OF SUFFERING AND
ONE HOUR OF BLISS

THE CENTER OF MY LIFE HAS ALWAYS BEEN
THE LOVE I HAVE BEEN GIVEN BY OTHERS

CONTENTS

FOREWORD

*T*he enterprise of asking prominent people what makes them tick began one late afternoon in the book stacks of an Austin library. I was poking around the shelves when my eyes fell on a book by the American philosopher-historian Will Durant entitled "On the Meaning of Life." Out of curiosity, I pulled it down and began scanning it for the answer to the ultimate question.

The book turned out to be a collection of letters. In 1932, Durant wrote a philosophical letter to 100 famous people, brazenly asking each the meaning of life. In response, Durant received answers from such notables as Theodore Dreiser, H. L. Mencken, Will Rogers, and Mahatma Gandhi. Although George Bernard Shaw snorted, "Does the question itself have meaning?", Durant maintained the question was particularly prescient in view of the gradual 20th Century buildup of economic, scientific, and technological changes that increased man's knowledge while undercutting his sense of importance.

In a burst of excitement, I felt compelled to contemporize Durant's book. I decided to carry Durant's spark of inquiry into the 1990s and send letters to people from all walks of life and throughout the world, seeking an answer to a vital question. Rather than using Durant's original question, "What is the meaning of life?" — which seemed too broad and metaphysical in scope — I devised my own. The question I decided to put to people was "What makes you tick?"

I submitted my idea to a test. I wrote Will Durant himself. One week later, to my utter surprise, Durant responded with a one-page, hand-typed answer. It was beautiful. I felt like an astronomer who has seen an old star shine with new brilliance.

Encouraged by his response, I sent a letter to several hundred people in different fields of endeavor.

Dear _____:

Will you interrupt your work for a moment to answer a personal, Boswellian question? Let me explain.

In 1932 the famous philosopher-historian Will Durant published an intriguing book entitled *On the Meaning of Life* in which he wrote to a hundred contemporaries in various walks of life asking them to tell what meaning life had for them. With a variation on his idea, I want to contemporize Mr. Durant's book.

Human beings live on meaning; we demand purpose. Such purpose is as important to us as food, security and sexual satisfaction. With this in mind, my question to you is: What makes *you* tick? What keeps you going? What is the goal or motive force of your toil? As the American historian Henry Adams wrote, "Everyone must bear his own universe, and most persons are moderately interested in learning how their neighbors have managed to carry theirs."

I posed the question to Mr. Durant, and in a recent personal correspondence he wrote to me, "I don't know if I tick, but what drives me on to work and marry and accept the usual tasks of life is the impulse to develop myself in perception, understanding, and expression—in a word to expand my Self. This is egoism but not necessarily egotism, which is self-exaggeration...".

You are a person whose work and intelligence I admire. What makes you tick? Would you let me use your answer in the book?

Your answer will mean very much to me personally.

Respectfully,

David Sharpe

A book about "what makes you tick?" suggests that it offers a formula for living life. But if I have learned anything from my correspondents, it is that there are as many formulas as there are people. Oliver Wendell Holmes wrote, "Life is painting a picture, not doing a sum." In other words, there is no single correct answer. To me, life isn't like a math problem, but rather a well-lived life is like a work of art, in that it should give a deeply-felt and enduring record of one's response to existence. We should paint what we are, paint what we believe, paint what we feel, not what is expected. If such a communication is unemotional and unenduring, then we are painting the life-picture with only our hands and not our hearts, producing something that is more an exercise and less a record which can stand the test of truth and time. A life worth living requires an artist's sense of the intangible, not an accountant's attachment to facts and figures. Life is not a cosmic theorem made up of numbers and equations.

This book will not paint the picture for the reader. But maybe these letters reproduced here will help bring the artist's colors into sharper focus and make us see the world before us with greater clarity.

*T*here is one fable that touches very near the quick of life: the fable of the monk who passed into the woods, heard a bird break into song, hearkened for a trill or two, and found himself on his return a stranger at his convent gates; for he had been absent fifty years, and of all his comrades there survived but one to recognise him. It is not only in the woods that this enchanter carols.... All life that is not merely mechanical is spun out of two strands: seeking for the bird and hearing him. And it is just this that makes life so hard to value, and the delight of each so incommunicable.

Robert Louis Stevenson
"The Lantern-Bearers"

TO EXPRESS THE UNIVERSE
DEPOSITED WITHIN US

*I*n his letter, Will Durant makes a useful distinction between egoism and egotism. The difference between the two words is as great as the difference between love and sex. Egoism, he writes, is self-expansion and self-satisfaction; egotism is self-exaggeration.

What makes us tick? What is the spine of a person's days? How should we live life? The answer to Durant and the correspondents in this section is to perform an act of "egoism": to become who we are, to overcome our feelings of inferiority and "express the universe deposited within us." Tom Clancy writes that the ultimate defense against growing old is to work to fulfill one's dream.

There is, however, a danger in thinking too much about one's ticking. We might end up like the centipede in the fable that starved to death because it could not decide which leg to use first. Ironically, we reach the highest pitch of fulfillment when we are so involved in work or with others that we forget ourselves totally and, for a time, escape the eggshell of our self-consciousness. To make this a habit and sustaining routine is a fundamental condition in the art of living.

Malcolm Cowley writes, "I want to capture the shape of my own life before it dissolves into mist. That effort keeps me going." That effort is what really matters, not being a success or achieving great things. And, if this idea smacks of overweening self-centeredness, consider this: in overcoming the birth pains that come from fashioning ourselves, we are also fashioning our part of the world.

Will Durant

Journalist, educator, American philosopher-historian and author (1885-1981), best known for his eleven-volume series, The Story of Civilization, much of which was written with his wife, Ariel Durant. The Durants gave nearly all their working hours (eight to fourteen daily) over four decades to complete the best-selling, monumental series on the cultural heritage of mankind.

I don't know if I tick, but what drives me on to work and marry and accept the usual tasks of life is the impulse to develop myself in perception, understanding, and expression—in a word, to expand my Self. This is egoism, but not necessarily egotism, which is self-exaggeration. I doubtless practice that too, but it is an accompaniment, not a basic drive. It is egoism—that is, self-satisfaction—not egotism, which is self-exaggeration. I have tried several times to analyze myself, and do not find much drive in a desire to surpass others; the drive seems to come from a restless urge to realize my own ideal of developing all my constructive capacities. Of course I never realize that goal, but I've been put to hard work by the dream.

George Burns

American comedian and popular entertainer in show business for over 80 years. At 87, the comic with the cigar, toupee and risque jokes, revealed part of his secret for a full and long life by publishing his ultimate diet, sex and exercise book, How to Live to be 100 — Or More.

What makes me tick? How do I know, I only went through the fourth grade, and I didn't pay too much attention even then.

I suppose what makes me tick is self-satisfaction. I love what I'm doing. And if I can also get a laugh, that thrills me. And if I don't get a laugh, I feel sorry for the people who missed the joke.

That's it, kid.

Christopher Fry

Eminent British playwright and Christian verse dramatist ("The Lady's Not For Burning" and "A Sleep of Prisoners"). Christopher Fry is also a distinguished translator-adaptor and a screenwriter (John Huston's "The Bible" and William Wyler's "Ben Hur"). However, his literary reputation seems to rest on his plays — a unique blend of verse and prose.

The most obvious answer to the question "What makes you tick?" is that the ticking heart puts us, willy-nilly, into the business of living. But I think your question really means: what importance do I put on the ticking? And there can be no single answer to that. There is the simple one, as I've written elsewhere, of being for an allotted span aware of the vast movement of a bewildering universe—a fascination ranging from the physical enjoyments it presents, to the dilemmas, challenges, sorrows and despairs it entails. In other words, to being part of the creative whole.

But there is also, I believe, a reality in the word Vocation, something within the creative purpose that "aims" us, whether or not we answer well to that aim. No one, as far as I know, has ever found a word for the shaping purpose of evolution. Darwin's "genetical change" and "natural selection" doesn't, it seems to me, really face up to the mystery, and no words, such as Mind or Will, can satisfy, either scientifically or imaginatively, the development of life; or of unconscious matter, come to that. Aren't we nearer discovery when we lay open our sensibilities to an intuitive exploration of what, though properly unnameable, we name 'God'? If you challenge me to say why I have written at all, my answer is that it was an effort, however inadequate, to express "the universe deposited within us." That sounds high-flown, so let me climb down to the simpler expectation of watching the seasons come and plants-planted grow: all that renewal at the garden which carries us along with.

Katherine Hepburn

*The only film actress to receive four Academy Awards for Best Performance by an Actress,
Katherine Hepburn is the "unchallenged first lady of American cinema."*

Heavens! I've no idea.
Good health and common sense I should imagine.

Sir Edmund Hillary

*On May 29, 1953, Sir Edmund Hillary, and the Nepalese Sherpa guide Tenzing Norgay, became the first
persons to climb and reach the summit of Mount Everest, the world's highest mountain. Following this,
Hillary took part in other expeditions. In 1958 he traveled overland to the South Pole, and later led a
jet boat expedition up the Ganges to establish the river's source. Along with being an adventurer, Hillary
is a builder of schools, bridges and hospitals high in the Himalayas for the Sherpas of Nepal.*

I'm damned if I know what makes me "tick". It's like trying to answer
the question "Why do you climb mountains?" The traditional answer
"because it is there" is probably as good a reason as any. I think I have
an urge to test myself against interesting challenges; to overcome things
even though they may terrify me; to prove to myself that I'm not as big
a failure as I suspect I may be—and by failure I mean not achieving the
full potential of which I may be capable.

Lendon H. Smith, M.D.

Known as "The Children's Doctor," pediatrician and nutritionist Dr. Lendon Smith is a pioneer in the area of nutrition in pediatrics. Through his numerous books and entertaining media appearances, Smith places particular emphasis on how diet and nutrition can keep children and adults healthy.

I suppose because you are a stranger to me, I can be perfectly frank. The more I work with the hyperactive child, the more I find that I am one of them. I have a strong need to win and to have everyone like me. I am never satisfied. I cannot delegate things to others well; I must do it all myself.

I am happiest when I am talking fast in front of a large audience and they are leaning forward, nodding their heads and taking notes.

Cheerful information is what I pass out. My father was a pediatrician; I have identified my life with his. He was so great.

I cannot relax and just stare into space without feeling guilty. I need to be productive. I also need to explore new and somewhat dangerous paths.

OK?

Mikhail Baryshnikov

World-renowned ballet dancer, choreographer and former director of the American Ballet Theatre. In addition to achieving complete mastery of the classical and contemporary dance repertory, Mikhail Baryshnikov has also found time to tackle the challenges of being a stage and screen actor.

If your question is, "what propels me in life?" then my answer is: I am grateful for the gifts which I have received and I feel especially responsible for those gifts. I feel that I have to, therefore, do my best...and try my utmost.

George Seldes

American jounalist and free press champion. Editor and publisher of In Fact, *a newsletter devoted to news often suppressed or dismissed by the general press. Throughout his life, George Seldes has conducted a vigorous campaign in support of freedom of the press and against the encroachment of fascism. He is the author of* Witness to a Century: Encounters with the Noted, the Nortorious, *and* the Three SOBs *and* The Great Thoughts.

Inasmuch as I never learned anything about genes and chromosomes, and next to nothing about heredity and environment, I concluded long ago, the middle 1920s when I worked in Vienna and attended regularly Alfred Adler's Wednesday (or was it Sunday?) afternoon teas and listened to him speak in a fatherly way about the behavior pattern - the phrase is his not mine - that my pattern was shaped, or cut, or whatever one does with patterns, in childhood by my father....

Father was a libertarian, a freethinker, a dissenter, an idealist—and incidentally a total failure. He was a founder or participant in at least five so-styled utopian colonies in New Jersey and New York. For the last, which he named "Belle Terre," he wrote a sort of "declaration of the rights of man," based on Tolstoyan principles, Kropotkin's "mutual aid," and Henry George's Single Tax as an economic system. Belle Terre never got off the ground.

Next to my father the person who influenced me most, and in a way directed the character of the work I was to do most of my life, was Dr. Adler of Vienna. Those wonderful afternoon teas. The mere mention of "the feeling of inferiority." He was considerably agitated when the press referred to him as "the *father* of the inferiority complex." "Complexes," he said, "are serious disorders; they require treatment. But the *feeling* of inferiority—every human being has a feeling of inferiority, and every one us must conquer it."

I remember the time he said it. I remember it as if it were a searchlight turned glaringly on all my sentient years, my struggle without knowing it with my own feeling of inferiority; and immediately, from that day on Dr. Adler's phrase began to change my life.

The first, and most important thing to do after the Adlerian experience, was to quit Col. McCormick's Tribune. Freelancing meant freedom.

Fortunately a new publisher wanted a book on censorship and suppression of news and fighting the dictators, and so I wrote "You Can't Print That." From then on, for about fifty years I have done what I could in my own field - I never founded a utopian colony or lived in one, but I devoted myself in seventeen or eighteen books and 520 issues of *In Fact*, to one subject: a free press in a free world. I have never asked myself why I have done what I did.

Thomas Berger

Along with Mark Twain, Thomas Berger is one of America's leading satirical novelists, best known for his novel Little Big Man. *Most of Berger's novels are a delicious mixture of satire, parody and black humor* (Neighbors, Arthur Rex).

Having had life imposed upon me without my consent, I have had one ruling purpose: to make existence interesting to myself.

Richard Eberhart

Pulitzer prize-winning American poet and longtime teacher, considered by critics and readers to be one of the major lyric and visionary poets of this century.

Your question would be answered if you read every poem I have written. The answer is implicit in the poetry. "Poetry is a recognition of man's estate and of his fate, and ultimately poetry is praise." I was asked for a statement by *Who's Who in America*. This is at the end of my account. I tell audiences about two different theories. One is of a split in the psyche at an early age. The poet creates to lave his psychic wound. It is a means of becoming whole. Another theory is that of exuberance.

A poet has more energy than to get from day to day and pours out his abundant spirit in art. There could be many more theories and I do not know that the above two (quite simply stated) are mutually exclusive.

Malcolm Cowley

Critic, poet, editor, translator, and influential figure in American letters (1898-1989), best known for his writings on William Faulkner and Exiles Return. Cowley's The Portable Faulkner (1946) virtually created a Faulkner literary revival when many of his books were out of print.

I want to capture the shape of my own life before it dissolves into mist. That effort keeps me going.

Raoul Berger

Authority of American constitutional law and history who wrote two ground-breaking studies on "impeachment" and "executive privilege" during President Nixon's administration. Berger, who is retired Charles Warren Senior Fellow in American legal history, Harvard Law School, is also a classical violinist.

I believe with Justice Holmes that life is "the use of one's powers, and that to use them to our height is our joy and duty."

In the beginning, when I sought to bend the violin to my will, self-expression was the goal, for music reaches into the depths of the soul. Later my preparation for the law introduced me to the joy of learning. There followed learning how to think; thinking said Dr. Johnson, is "a process of discovery which has its own pleasures." For me, to develop a fresh insight, to crack a problem, has been an abiding joy, subsequent approval, if any, being merely frosting on the cake.

Richard Wilbur

*Pulitzer prize-winning American poet, and one of the premier translators of his generation.
With Lillian Hellman, Richar Wilbur wrote the libretto for the Opera "Candide."*

I am kept going by the pleasure of doing what I do well: writing poems, raising herbs, translating. And I am also made happy by much that I do indifferently well: cycling, dancing, swimming, cooking. None of these things would matter, however, without love, friendship, and a sense of usefulness and interaction.   For all my self-centered talk of doing, I know that I am most alive when I forget myself totally — in work, or with others, or in a natural world that is mysterious but quite real and not alien.

Walter Jackson Bate

*One of America's great humanists and literary scholars. Walter Jackson Bate is a professor of English and
author of critically acclaimed biographies on John Keats and Samuel Johnson. Bate has long been
famous for his vivid narrative style and his insight in using psychology to illuminate literature.*

I'm sorry I can't give you an answer to what "motivates" me. I suppose I could if I were referring to myself in my 20s, 30s, or even 40s. Then it was somewhat similar to what you quote from Will Durant. I'd phrase it differently: "The desire to understand human nature especially through its literature, but also through philosophy, psychology, and history."

But, sometimes, as people get older, they begin to feel that knowledge is inexhaustible — that, no matter how far you go, you still seem almost equally remote; and you know you're not going to get any final answers.

In that case, the motivation that remains is sheer *habit*. I go on doing the things I do (teaching and writing about literature) because I'm used to it and, in my 60s, it's not likely for circumstances to change.

12

David L. Miller

Philosopher and educator David Miller (1903-1986) was a leading authority on George Herbert Mead, the social psychologist and philosopher with whom he studied at the University of Chicago. Miller, an expert on theories of knowledge and the philosophy of science, taught and wrote books on philosophy until his retirement at the University of Texas at Austin after a 44-year career.

Lower animals live by instinct and impulses and are motivated only by what is immediate in experience, by responding to their immediate feelings of hunger, pain, sex, etc. But human beings are motivated, in addition, by what lies ahead, by a conception of what is not present but what they hope can be reached through their own effort, the motive force.

In general, it is not money, profit, material goods that motivates a healthy minded person, but rather, a better image (conception) of himself in his own eyes and in the eyes of members of his group or community.

You want to know what motivates me. I spoke generally, and now if you ask, What motivates yourself, I believe it is not finally to know about me so much as to write or publish something of which you can be proud—so as to create a better image of yourself ....

Probably shame, guilt and conscience are the great controllers and stabilizers of individual conduct. They help, in every case, determine the particular ends we choose (or the particular motives) as well as the means. And no one can have self-respect, or take pride in his achievements unless he believes others approve. (In some cases people say God approves.) The great partner of every individual is that "still small voice" of the community or of the great and ever present Companion.

Now a healthy minded person can never rest on his laurels. The self is that which must ever transcend itself. Though he "takes a licking, he must keep on ticking." But one is most fortunate if every particular goal that is reached can be used as a means to still greater achievement, believing that a bird in the bush is worth two in the hand.

Though we are many, we are severally members of a sea of selves that sustains each of us in thoughtful choice and its implementation.

Denis de Rougemont

A noted Swiss writer and publisher (1906-1985), became a leading advocate of European unity. In 1939, Denis de Rougement gained international attention with his philosophical Love in the Western World *in which he analyzed the roots of passion. All told, he wrote 30 books and his work has been translated into 17 languages.*

The goal of my life is to discover the goal of my life—my calling—and to conform my judgements and plans to it better and better. The calling comes to me from elsewhere; not from the subconscious but from the supreme conscious and nothing, neither science nor reason, can guarantee me its authenticity if it itself doesn't.

Starting off from a place without precedent—as I myself do—I tend toward the Absolute Goal, common to all. But each person must *invent his footpath* toward that End of all human ethics. "If the end doesn't justify the means, then what does?" an American philosopher said to me one evening in Venice. This was illuminating for me.

For the path creates itself under the steps which follow it. "Your Word is a lamp unto my feet, a light unto my path." To dare to go forward into the night towards a goal, through imagined time, to place one's foot on what could very well be emptiness; such is faith, which is "certainty of things hoped for, firm assurance of those one does not see." (Hebrews XI, 1)

Now, I know that my calling, which is, like all others, unique and without precedent, becomes true only in the style of my work and through my life in the community of my fellow beings. Where I've taken not only an ethic but a whole policy, and my "involvement," from, the answer is from myself, since 1934—in the service of a society organized in a federation of regions, the region being the community unit in which a man's voice may carry.

Erma Bombeck

Through her numerous best-selling books and weekly newspaper columns, which are syndicated in over one thousand newspapers, Erma Bombeck trains a side-splitting and satirical eye on the foibles of the middle class lifestyle.

Your asking me to do something that I rarely do...dissect what I'm all about. I've always thought it robbed one of spontaneity and didn't make much sense to anyone else, but here goes.

WHAT MAKES ERMA BOMBECK TICK?

"I thrive on some of the greatest "non virtues" in the world: impatience with myself, a mammoth insecurity in what I do, and I'm possessed by a drive to please.

"It's curious but I don't expect nearly as much out of me in my private life as I do professionally. I have no personal goals, no great driving force and willingly forgive my inadequacies.

"But in front of a typewriter, I never ask. I demand! It's like a game sometimes to tackle a challenge just to see if I can pull it off. I don't know how much potential is there, but I will never live with myself until I have given it my best shot.

"The writer Bombeck needs the private Bombeck to function far more than the private Bombeck needs...the writer."

Isaac Asimov

Known as the "great explainer" for his articulate elucidation of technical subjects, Isaac Asimov is the successful author of an incredible output of science fiction and nonfiction material (twenty million words in print, including more than 320 books). With his broad knowledge, Asimov has tackled a wide range of topics in his nonfiction books and has become admired for handling fiction and nonfiction with equal proficiency.

I don't know if my answer would be useful to you. I am not given to inner probings or self-analysis. As far as I know, I work because I am doing what I enjoy and I am a weak-willed character who only likes to do what he enjoys.

Tom Clancy

With the publication of his bestselling and highly acclaimed The Hunt for Red October, *Tom Clancy joined the front ranks of the world's thriller writers. His subsequent books have shown he is a master of what one critic labeled the "technico-military thriller".*

Some years ago I found myself in a contemplative mood that comes to us all at least once per day, and I asked myself a question that I must have asked thousands of times:

What do you want to be when you grow up?

It hit me then that I was well over thirty. I had home, and the mortgage that goes along with it. Two cars, and the car payments that go along with them. Two children, and the responsibilities that accrue to them, also. I was in a job that had its good moments and bad, and whether I liked it or not, I knew that I could not afford to leave it for the reasons already ennumerated.

The stunning, and depressing realization hit me that I was grown up, finally, and while I might not be what I wanted to be, I was in the middle-class trap that I myself had forged just as surely Scrooge's partner, Jacob Marley, had forged his own chains of destiny. It hit me that I would have to get along as best I could, making my payments, fulfilling my responsibilities, worrying about the future as most of us learn to do.

I had quite seriously planned on staying young forever, but it came to me a few years ago that somehow I had failed, and it had all caught up with me. There were compensations: a wife I love, my children, good friends, and a fairly comfortable life — but it was not a pleasant realization to know that my options were effectively at an end. It was less pleasant to realize that there was no one to be blamed but myself.

Thank God — I was wrong. There was a way out of the trap. It took me a few more years of dabbling to find it, but it was always there, waiting to be rediscovered.

Each of us has a dream — something you want to accomplish for yourself. The ultimate defense against growing old is your dream.

Nothing is as real as a dream. The world can change, but your dream will not. Life may change, but your dream doesn't have to, because the dream is within you. No one can take your dream away.

16

The only way that your dream can die is if you kill it yourself. If you do that, you will have condemned yourself along with it. You will never be able to blame another for that. Failure, like success, is something that you will make for yourself. You will always have that choice.

Success isn't money. At most, money is nothing more than a convenient way to keep score. Success isn't power. Power is an illusion. The criteria for your success are to be found in your dream, in your self. These criteria are called ideals, and as they are the substance of dreams, so also is their achievement the definition of success.

It is within the power of each of us to fulfill that dream.

Your dream is the best expression of your self. Your dream is something to hold onto. It will always be your link with the person you are today, young and full of hope. If you hold onto it, you may grow old, but you will never be old. And that is the ultimate success.

Bob Kane

The artist who created the caped crusader, Batman. Now approaching his seventies,
Bob Kane invented Batman in 1939 when he was eighteen;
he drew the character and wrote the stories for DC Comics from 1939 to 1966.

A myriad of profound philosophies I have absorbed during my lifetime studying with several wise sages in the world has given me one universal truth which I live by. And that is summed up in one world — *Creativity*.

My entire life has been filled and fulfilled with my insatiable penchant to be a creative entity. It is my intrinsic feeling that life gives all persons an innate creative potential to fulfill in order to find real inner contentment. Every man must have a mission in life, however big or small, to justify his existence. Otherwise without a mission he has no motivation to greet each new day and will wind up being an unfulfilled empty shell.

Luckily for me I discovered my mission and creativity early in life through my obsessive desire to be creative and have followed it through to its successful fruition. Words cannot express how spiritually rewarding it has been for me by fulfilling my childhood dream to become a successful cartoonist.

Batman is my crowning achievement and proves how far one can go from humble beginnings if he has the perception, tenacity, perseverance and determination to reach one's goal in spite of road-blocks detouring the chosen path along the way.

And that partially sums up what makes Bob Kane "tick" — to be *creative* each and every day be it drawing, painting or writing or just meditating on one more creative mountain to climb in my attempt to top Mt. Everest.

John Callahan

The "Alfred Hitchcock of cartooning." A quadriplegic (as a result of a car accident at 21) and recovered alcoholic, John Callahan draws cartoons that poke fun at alcoholics, the handicapped, even the dead. His work has appeared in Omni, Penthouse, Harpers, and other magazines and is syndicated in eighteen newspapers. His recently published autobiography is entitled Don't Worry, He Won't Get Far On Foot.

I feel I have a special calling. When I do the work I was born to do, I get a sense of fullfilment. That keeps me going. My goal is to make the most of the life I was given. I accept the challenge of my disability, realizing that my potential is in no way limited by it. I'm constantly asked by people if I have any idea why I've had to suffer so much. And I answer that I guess the reason for all human suffering is to make us better harmonica players.

Hazel Henderson

Internationally known futurist, economist, adviser to many government and citizen—organizations, and video producer. Hazel Henderson is, as William Irwin Thompson says, "one of a small number who can take ideas, visions, and new paradigms and make them understood. She is a true transformer in more ways than one." She is the author of The Politics of the Solar Age *and* Creating Alternative Futures.

Your question is my favorite one. My passion in life is to become as whole as possible — so as to relate to more fully to the wholeness of this marvelous creation.

Life is such a great gift and what makes it so is this search for deeper meaning and relatedness.

At this time, the planet clearly has taken over as the primary teacher of all humans — providing us with all the positive and negative feedback we need to nudge us along toward great awareness and wisdom.

Paul R. Ehrlich

Paul Ehrlich is a world-renowned ecologist and leader in the international crusade for population control and ecological awareness. Over the years, he has been near the center of debate over global warming, biodiversity, nuclear winter and science education. Currently Bing Professor of Population Studies and Professor of Biology at Stanford University, Ehrlich has authored over 400 scientific articles and more than 20 books. His latest book, which he co-wrote with his wife Anne, is titled The Population Explosion.

To earn and keep the respect of my colleagues, to believe that I've helped to make the world a little better place (both obviously involved in ego satisfaction), and to thoroughly enjoy life.

John Henry Faulk

*Folksy Texas humorist who became popular in the 1950s on national radio and
early television as a storyteller (1913-1990). The most important story he told, however, was his own
First Amendment struggle against the 1950's anti-Communist blacklisting practice
in the entertainment industry. The story of the $3.5 million libel judgment he won against
Aware, Inc., the group that blacklisted Faulk and other entertainers for alleged Communist ties,
is described in his 1964 book Fear On Trial.*

That which gives my life meaning, that makes me so keen to stay alive
and find what tomorrow might bring, is my having achieved, despite my
many limitations and flaws, a genuine affection and respect for my own
worth.

Dame Joan Sutherland

*One of the first ladies of opera, Joan Sutherland is the world's pre-eminent coloratura soprano.
One critic wrote, "She has, quite simply, the most beautiful voice in the world."
In addition to becoming the undisputed sovereign of the bel canto repertory,
Sutherland also helped further the careers of those who went on to be major stars,
including Luciano Pavarotii, Marilyn Horne and James Morris.
Unpretentious and cheerful, Sutherland is now retired and quite happy, she says,
to stay at home in Switzerland and work in her garden.*

In a nutshell, what makes me "tick" is the desire to realize to the full
the gifts and talents with which I have been bestowed and plough them
back into the world at large. I also gain great satisfaction from our earth's
natural beauties.

I WANT TO KNOW THE TRUTH
ABOUT EVERYTHING

*C*uriosity led Eve to bite the apple and Pandora to open the box. Curiosity, not sin, is the original itch and the urge to scratch it, say the myths, opened the way to sorrow and suffering — and boredom.

For these correspondents, however, curiosity is the greatest virtue and killing it a far graver sin than any committed by Pandora or Eve. For them the search for the meaning is the meaning. Like detectives sifting through the evidence, each is constantly searching for clues to resolve some mystery or question. Nor will they rest until they've found the answer. Colin Turnbull searches for why good things sometimes emerge from ugly and irrational situations. Colin Wilson suspects that inside each of us is "a robot," a behavioral mechanism that fosters passivity and despair. Physicist John Archibald Wheeler says he's willing to go to any lengths to find out "how this strange and beautiful world is put together." Brooks Atkinson, at 85, continued to be involved with politics, literature, and drama to see if "life is improving for everyone or falling behind." For each, curiosity is the advancing edge of light into life's dark recesses.

Paradoxically, the answers they find only unlock other mysteries. The curious mind, however, is not stopped. Its appetite is insatiable, just as the knowledge it seeks is inexhaustible.

John C. Lilly, M.D.

*John C. Lilly has been described as "one of the pathbreaking explorers of that great
terra incognita, the human brain." Noted for his studies of human-dolphin communication
(to determine the possibility of communication between man and other species),
Lilly has also been an explorer in various other fields of science, including
biophysics, neurophysiology and electronics.*

You asked the question, "What makes me tick?"   I take in that question
that the "makes me" is not a physiological question and that the "tick"
is not a valve slap in my heart. I don't know whether Toni [a dolphin]
agrees, but I seem to be mostly motivated by curiosity about the mind,
the brain, the spirit and sexual differences between these entities.

I truly appreciate how totally ridiculous the condition of me and all
other humanity is and how we insist on increasing the nonsense which
we feed one another.

P.S. I don't normally answer letters such as yours but due to my present
seductive and entrancing present circumstances with Toni and Molly, I did.

Claude Lévi-Strauss

*Internationally known French social anthropologist, founder of structural anthropology
and author of numerous books, including* The Savage Mind *and the* Raw and the Cooked.
L'evi-Strauss has been described as one of the major architects of the thought of our times.

What makes me "tick," as you say, is a daily struggle against boredom.
And trying to understand things that I don't understand, even with no
success, is the only way out of that predicament that I have found so far.

Brooks Atkinson

For thirty-five years the most influential voice in American drama belonged to New York Times critic Brooks Atkinson (1894-1984). His theatre reviews determined the fate of plays appearing on Broadway, Off-Broadway and ultimately the whole American stage. Atkinson was also a journalist who was awarded the Pulitzer Prize in 1947 for his foreign reporting on the Soviet Union.

In answer to your inquiry I have to begin by saying that I am 85 years old and not in good health at present. What my life means at present is that I am in the mood to reach the end of it.

All my life, and including today, I have chiefly been concerned with journalism and now that I am retired I spend about two hours every morning reading the news. I am concerned with politics, literature, and drama and I read books consistently. I am concerned with having enough background to develop an intelligent and humane attitude towards life and to have some idea whether life is improving for everyone or falling behind.

George Gaylord Simpson

George Gaylord Simpson's work on vertebrate paleontology contributed greatly to the understanding of evolution and earned the scientist a reputation as one of the world's foremost authorities on evolutionary theory. Describing himself primarily as an earth scientist, Simpson (1902-1984) was as much a philosopher of organismic biology as a careful researcher of fossil mammals.

The question as to what makes some one tick is ambiguous. Surely for anyone there are many quite different things that make him or her tick in some sense of this expression. For me a major source of drive or motive force can be most simply expressed as *curiosity*. From the time of my earliest memories right into my present old age my curiosity has been insatiable. I was and am interested in practically everything, and I always wanted and still want to *know* as much as I can, while recognizing that I cannot know everything, not even all things I judge important. This drive carried me through many long years of schooling, from kindergarten to a doctorate, and then through longer years—well over half a century so far—of a career in science. The discovery in my teens that I could not only learn things new to me but also discover things new to everyone made it inevitable that I would become a scientist. The breadth of my curiosity also ensured that although I did much concentrated technical research even that spread so that it involved both the physical sciences and the life sciences. Marginal to my professional research, my curiosity also lead me into such diverse things as linguistics, history, philosophy, architecture, art, and on and on.

Another thing that has made me tick has been a severe case of caoethes scribendi, contracted in grade school and still raging. This is related to the curiosity drive, for I have wanted to convey what I have learned to others and I prefer to do this in writing. Much is reporting on new results of research, but much also is an effort to interpret and to arouse and to appease curiosity in wider, less technical circles. I have just made entry 744 in my bibliography, which is a new book on a scientific subject but written for intelligent nonscientists.

Still another drive, also in the complex centering around curiosity has been a love for nature, for the wonders of the world, for going to see them in every hemisphere, on all continents, and across all seas and oceans.

A thing that has made and does make me tick, but that does not center on curiosity is love. It certainly has included sex, but is a far broader emotion. I dearly love my wife, my children, and my grandchildren. I have also loved and still do love many others, women, men, and children.

So what else has made me tick? Dozens of things, beyond the space for mention here.

Carleton S. Coon

Considered one of the last great general anthropologists, Carleton S. Coon (1904-1981) made contributions to many areas of the science. He studied the social anthropologies of contemporary societies, but his main interest was ancient man and the anthropological study of human history.

It had never occurred to me to think about what makes me tick until last week when I found a letter from a publisher of mine dated about eight years ago in which he was rejecting my autobiography. He said there was no evidence of it in my MS. Then I began to wonder. The point is, I have always been too busy.

Now I have a beginning of an idea.

I have always thought of things outside myself, and what makes other people, groups of people, races, cultures, events in history, life itself, the earth, the planets, and the forces of nature tick.

That is why I have travelled as much as I have been able, studied people and tried to trace their origins in caves.

Just call me a generalist, not a specialist, a lover of the Earth and all its peoples and, above all, justice.

I hope that you will not think that this is boasting.

Colin Wilson

For over 30 years Colin Wilson has concerned himself with a reexamination of modern philosophy and how to achieve a richer spiritual life for man. Wilson has written in many literary fields, including nonfiction, novels and scholarly investigations of crime and the occult.

Thanks for your interesting letter.

Human beings are inclined to make a natural assumption that they do not possess very much freedom. If for example you wake up in the middle of the night and begin worrying, you have a clear picture of your-self as a fairly passive entity, at the mercy of 'fate' or mere circumstance.

On the other hand—and this is what interests me—we are always getting curious moments in which we become absolutely certain that human beings possess *far more* freedom then they ever realise. I remember a student once describing to me the feeling of arriving in London for a University interview, and walking down the Edgware Road with a feeling that life was suddenly opening up, and that everything that would happen would be absolutely fascinating—no matter how difficult or unpleasant! In these moods, we have the feeling that our normal state of mind is somehow poor and low-spirited, and that it simply fails to take account of the immense possibilities of human existence—as if we'd simply got stuck in a rut and were unable to grasp that it is perfectly easy to get out of. In my teens, I was excited by the remark in *Mr. Polly*—'If you don't like your life you can change it.'

I have always been convinced that this freedom exists, and that we can claim it with a certain amount of effort and courage. All we have to do is to call the bluff of this sensation that life is limited and boring.

You could say that all my work is an attempt to *analyse* why this sensation seems so convincing as long as we are actually feeling it. It is partly to do with what I call 'the robot'—the part of us that learns to do things automatically, and which unfortunately takes over a great deal of the functions that we should be doing with effort. This is the major culprit—the cause of what Gurdjieff calls our 'sleep.'

Sartre wrote *Being and Nothingness* to analyse his sense of the meaninglessness of human existence. You could say that all of my work is a similar kind of analysis of my own sense of the meaning of human existence. It is, I think an extremely precise analysis, and I feel that I'm rather like a detective going around with a magnifying glass endlessly looking for the slightest clues. I suppose you could call my books—*The Outsider* to *Mysteries*—a collections of clues.

Georges Simenon

*World-renowned Belgian writer of more than 200 mysteries,
psychological novels and detective stories (1903-1989). His most famous creation
is Inspector Jules Maigret of the Paris police force who rarely carries a gun, rarely throws
a punch or takes one and is seldom involved in a chase either on foot or by car.*

I spent the greatest part of my life trying to understand the human animal such as he is in himself, naked, without the rags in which he has been parading over the centuries in order to get over his apprehensions or to dominate. Now, at sixty-eight, I wonder whether his anguishes were not born the day his pride made him add to his name the word "sapiens".

Harrison Salisbury

One of the most distinguished foreign correspondents for the New York Times. During his five-decade career Harrison Salisbury has roved the international scene. His farther travels have taken him to Russia, Siberia, Central Asia, Outer Mongolia, China, Tibet, North Korea and Southeast Asia. His reports on Russia brought Salisbury his widest acclaim (his Times series, "Russia Reviewed," won the 1955 Pulitizer Prize) and established him as dean of Kremlin-watchers. After retiring from the New York Times Salisbury has published books on China, America, a history of the Times, and his own life story.

I was born with an insatiable curiosity to find out what makes things tick. As a child I took things apart to the despair of my father and mother. In adult life I have devoted myself to more complex tasks, finding out what makes the world tick — Russia, China, the USA. You name it. Why and what lies at the root of racial violence. What is inside Mr. Nixon? Why do we vote for Ike and not for Adlai? What is Communism? Does it exist? What are the leaders really like — Stalin, Mao, Deng, Gorbachev, Bush. Things like that. The older I get the more curious I am. If I tick it is because I want to know why.

Linus Pauling

Eminent American scientiest in the fields of biochemistry, biology, physics, and genetics. Recipient of the Nobel Prize in Chemistry (1954) and the Nobel Peace Prize (1962) for his personal crusade against nuclear warfare and nuclear testing.

My curiosity about the nature of the world and my pleasure in making discoveries.

Arthur C. Clarke

Arthur C. Clarke is best known as the world's most commercially successful and highly respected contemporary science fiction writer. His imagination has taken his readers to the farthest reaches of outer space and time in such books as The City and the Stars, A Fall of Moondust, and 2001: A Space Odyssey and countless articles, books and short stories. Clarke regards science fiction not as escapism but the only kind of writing that deals with real problems and possibilities.

I think I can answer with one word — curiosity!

Colin M. Turnbull

With the publications of his two well-known anthropological works, The Forest People (1961) and The Mountain People (1972), Colin Turnbull has become known as one of the world's leading social anthropologists whose rigorous scientific field research is matched by a profound humanistic concern for the ways of different peoples.

Obviously one thing that makes me tick is a nagging conscience, something that makes me commit myself to do certain things, and having committed myself then compels me (ultimately!) to do them...in most cases. I am still trying to learn not to overcommit myself, and to say "no" at the outset rather than to have to back out of a commitment, which has happened once or twice to my dismay and to the inconvenience of others.

But what is the source of this conscience? Morality? Belief? Those would be non-answers. "Faith" comes closer; an absolute conviction, beyond reason, a certainty, that something is so or should be so. The recognition of such an article of faith, for me, is on the one hand transformed into a quest at the rational level...it becomes a hypothesis (or a plain hunch) to be tested; and there what makes me tick is an insatiable curiosity. I want to know everything...or perhaps better, I want to know the truth about everything, regardless of what the truth proves to be. Of course I know I can never know anything but a microscopic fraction of what there is to be known, which is where my "other hand" approach comes, so I have to select where to invest my energy...and I do that not according to any rational ordering and ranking of moral priorities, but according to the intensity of that initial perception. I am convinced that there is some human significance in the fact that some people prefer to drink beer from glasses and others from bottles and others from cans and others from cans wrapped in brown paper bags (even under lawful situations), and some while driving. I would love to know what makes these people tick in these particular kinds of ways because they are ways in which human beings relate to each other, for better or worse. So I would rank this possible avenue of inquiry above my curiosity about why holly and pine shed in such inconvenient ways, but below why racism seems to be such a dominant feature of modern civilization.

So I tick most vigorously when human relations are concerned, and when I observe consistency in behavioral patterns...i.e. individual or isolated behaviour does not arouse my curiosity as much as group, institutionalised behaviour. That is my anthropological training...the social process grabs me far more strongly than the individual process.

So, still at the rational level, inconsistency makes me tick, with vehemence rather than vigour...perhaps because it is essentially irrational. And one of the greatest inconsistencies of our time is the divorce between what we preach and what we practice. That is structural lunacy, if not suicide.

On the other hand, the recognition of an article of faith, the immediate and direct perception of what appears in the form of an absolute truth, opens up another avenue of exploration, and alternative to the necessity for rigorous rational investigation and testing. It is the path of the mystic, a path that is equally rigorous, a path that investigates and tests, probing just as deeply as any rational process. I wish I was more skilled..or had more courage...or whatever, so that I could devote more time and energy in this direction, because it satisfies me even more deeply than the rational process, and somehow replaces the enormous amount of energy it consumes. So, again, I tick with enthusiasm and appreciation...and perhaps a little envy...when I am brought face to face with non-rational behaviour; that is a very different thing from the irrational behaviour that sends me up the wall...a totally useless waste of energy. So, I tick when I see this intuitive process at work, because it comes as close to perfection as anything I know...an unexpected, totally unpredictable, but somehow *necessary* act of kindness or compassion or consideration...that is a gem of perfection that outshines any triumph of reason, for me...and I tick with more than enthusiasm, more with joy, if not ecstacy, when it unfolds fully...as when, during a murder trial in North Carolina, the mother of the murderer found herself next to the mother of (the) young victim. At first the rational process prevailed, in the form of irrationality...a senseless hostility hatred, a violence that was almost tangible. Then both simple, uneducated, good women took the alternative path, and out of all that misery something good resulted. And goodness in human relations, however we arrive at it, makes me tick more than anything.

John Wheeler

A pioneer among twentieth century physicists. Noted for inventing the term "black hole," one of the more fascinating theories in astrophysics, which Wheeler developed as a result of his theoretical work on gravitational collapse, unified field theory and space-time continuum. Wheeler was also involved in the Manhattan Project, which developed the atom bomb, and he later participated in the theoretical work that finally led to the development of the first hydrogen bomb in 1952.

What keeps me going (at 79) faster than ever, you ask. "To find out how this strange and beautiful world is put together. I'm willing to go anywhere, see anyone, ask any questions, make a fool of myself a hundred times over, if it will help make headway with this great question.

And when we do get the answer, it will surely be so simple, so beautiful, so compelling, that we will all say to each other, 'Oh how could we have been so blind so long.'"

Sir Peter Hall

Probably no one has had greater impact on the British theatre of the last two decades than Peter Hall. He is founder of the Royal Shakespeare Company, former director of Britain's National Theatre and a director of films and many renowned theatre and opera productions in England and New York. Most recently Hall directed Dustin Hoffman as Shylock in Shakespeare's The Merchant of Venice.

I believe in intelligence and asking the right questions until you achieve a credible answer. I believe in tolerance, compassion and co-operation. All of this is why I am a director: a good day's work makes the individual actors and me better than we really are.

I believe in *knowing* and I believe in the theatre as a live help to knowing.

All the other rewards — success, money, power, status — are only helps to continue the work. They are of no lasting value in themsleves.

Madeleine L'Engle

A writer who has successfully published plays, poems, essays, an autobiography, and novels for both children and adults. Praised as one of the finest of present-day authors writing for young people, Madeleine L'Engle is probably best known for her trilogy of children's books, A Wrinkle in Time, A Wind in the Door, *and* A Swiftly Tilting Planet. *These novels blend science fiction, fantasy and profound moral questions.*

I was born into a storytelling family and wrote my first story when I was five years old, and have been writing and reading stories ever since because the story is the human being's chief vehicle of truth.

Vincent Price

A star of stage and screen since the age of twenty-four, Vincent Price has come to be best known for his roles in such horror classics as The Masque of the Red Death, House of Wax and Theatre of Blood. Price received acclaim in 1978 for his portrayal of Oscar Wilde in the one-man show, Diversions and Delights. From 1983 to 1989 he served as host of "Mystery," the syndicated PBS series. Price is also a knowledgeable collector of fine art.

The very fact that I'm still ticking must be proof that I've kept some kind of Time with my self and Time itself. Looking back, and still keeping an eye on the future, I think, nay, I know, it can all be summed up in one word — Curiosity! What makes others tick, especially in the Arts', is what makes me — tick!

I AM BUT THE SMALLEST OF COGS,
PART OF AN IMMENSE
UNIVERSAL CLOCK

*T*hey use such terms as "The Great Tradition," "evolution," "an immense universal clock," or "the ancient primordial qualities of the land." Each sees himself or herself as part of a larger whole, an active cell in the body of life. And because they do, some are driven by a strong sense of destiny about their work, as Jane Goodall is in her study of the chimpanzees; while others, like Wallace Stegner, feel compelled to do what they can to leave the world "a microgram of enhanced humanity." Believing in an ultimate Creator, Richard Nelson Bolles writes that "the purpose of life is to live always, hour by hour, in consciousness of His presence, and in gratitude for this gift" (life). Meanwhile, A.B. Gunthrie, Jr. writes, "I am not a religious person, but I have the compulsion to account to unknown gods, and I keep trying."

The message of these individuals is that we are not godlike; we can never be self-sufficient human islands independent of the outer world. Our living is contingent upon silent and unseen forces outside and beyond our private egos: forces that act very much like a passionate and demanding teacher who defines the questions and challenges the students beyond their limits, beyond even the endurance of Job, but then leaves to his class to decide how they will respond — with courage and concern or despair and indifference.

At such moments, we need something greater than our own self-confidence to fall back on, something that begins with imagination, transcends fear, and ends with faith.

Jane Goodall, Ph.D.

*Ethologist and one of the world's most respected and best-known experts on the behavior of
chimpanzees and other primates. Goodall was also one of the first to conduct
extensive research on wild chimpanzees in their natural habitat, which ultimately led her to make
important discoveries in the field of animal behavior.*

I don't think I can really answer your question as to what makes me
tick. There are too many levels. I mean—one lives from day to day
because the human animal, like other animals, is programmed to survive
—to develop, mature, reproduce, care for his or her young. And, since
I had a child, one very strong motivation in my life has been to care for
him, to see him grow into a responsible and independent adult.

On another level, what motivates my work? There are several totally
different answers. Firstly, part of my work is out in the field observing
the chimpanzees. To be alone with them in the forests, or even just in
the forests, makes much of the rest of my life worth while. The feeling
I have, at such times, of peace and the eternal nature of things gives me
strength to cope with the rough patches in life and the slogging of data
analysis. At a different level, ever since I began working on the chimpanzees I have felt a strong feeling of destiny: that this work is my allotted
task and that I must keep on with it because no one else will. And, again,
I carry on because I love the work and because I am absolutely and utterly
consumed with curiosity so that each additional year of work is pure
self-gratification. And I love to share the knowledge with others—put
it across. Probably a similar drive to that which motivates a missionary!

Last of all, I do believe in a God and a life hereafter. That, probably,
is one of the strongest mechanisms which keeps my ticking strong and even!

Wallace Stegner

Through such works as The Big Rock Candy Mountain *and the Pulitzer Prize-winning* Angel of Repose, *Wallace Stegner has established himself as one of America's most important living novelists and devoted students of the American West. As a writer with interests also in history, biography and conservation, Stegner has made many valuable contributions to American letters.*

I *know* what makes me tick: work. And what makes me work seems to be a dim belief, never fully articulated—call it a faith—that somehow, far off, some good may fall. With all the evidence of the cussedness, greed, and selfishness of the human race, I have to remember also the evidence of its occasional nobility, its endless curiosity, its yearning for good even when it is engaged in doing ill. I'd like to believe, and probably do, that the lifelong effort of good men and women doesn't simply get swallowed up in the general lava flow of ignorance, ill will, and self-ishness. It does, ultimately, leaven the lump: that is what we call the Great Tradition. That is what lets us learn, however painfully and slowly, from one age to another. I would like to be one of those who have learned a little during my life. I would like to be among those who have left the world a grain of understanding, a morsel of good feeling, a microgram of enhanced humanity. That is the highest ambition I can conceive of, and I am by no means sure I haven't elected myself to a company where I don't belong. But how do you climb without taking hold of a rung?

Conversely, I don't much value the things our mass media advertise and our therapists prescribe. Pleasure seems to me a splendid byproduct and a contemptible goal. Money I value only enough to let me live in reasonable comfort. Power I am suspicious of, because in all my life I never saw it used with full integrity. I believe with Henry Adams that a friend in power is a friend lost; and with Lord Acton that power tends to corrupt, and absolute power tends to corrupt absolutely, and with Winston Churchill that democracy is the worst sort of government, except all the others. So I content myself with trying to be a responsible citizen and a dependable friend and a man whose principles stand at least an inch further above the water than his temptations. And I try to examine my life and the life I see around me, and to write it as I see it.

James J. Lynch, Ph.D.

Leading American specialist in psychosomatic medicine. James J. Lynch is a psychologist and Co-Director of the Psychophysiological Clinic and Laboratories at the University of Maryland School of Medicine. He is also the author of the widely acclaimed The Broken Heart: the medical consequences of loneliness.

In terms of what makes me tick, I suppose it's not the "what" that even concerns me, but the "who?" I run on the assumption that there is a God, who oversees the universe and that He makes it all tick. To that extent I am but the smallest of small cogs, part of an immense universal clock that keeps astoundingly precise time. In that context, what makes me tick is love of life, which fortunately has permeated every part of my life.

John Pfeiffer

American scholar and popular writer of anthropology, archeology and science, with a special focus on prehistory and the future of human evolution; author of The Emergence of Man, The Emergence of Society (1977) and The Creative Explosion (1982). Due to his ability to clarify complex technical ideas, Pfeiffer's books can be an intellectual adventure for everyone.

In a nutshell what keeps me going and thinking is faith, humanistic faith that we are becoming saner, not unfortunately for moral reasons but by the sheer force of evolution. The sort of society implied by "getting saner" is something that none of us, radical and reactionary and everything in between, will like. But that of course is a poor standard.

What is continually exciting is the struggle to learn, and the struggle within oneself against the almost compulsive feeling that one has already learned. It is a great temptation to play the expert, the pontiff, a temptation fed by admirers, the most dangerous thing a person can have if he wants to keep growing as long as possible. The minute one begins to say and to feel "this is the way it is, take it from me" one is through as a thinker. But, again, this is something to fight against and never lower your guard!

Learning is fun, the source of continual excitement and awareness, but it has a lot more going for it than that. If there is to be peace, order, security, Eden, call it what you will, we must create it—and that calls for successive hypotheses, particularly in the study of human evolution and the social sciences.

We know a great deal about atoms, almost as much about cells and simple organisms, and alchemically little about ourselves. The next big advance to look forward to is the breakthrough in self-understanding which is not so far away and will hurt because it will be finishing what Copernicus started and will represent a new evolutionary emergence.

Patrick Moore

To the general public, Patrick Moore is astronomy's Baedeker to the night sky. A highly respected British astonomer, Moore is one of the most prolific authors of popular astronomy (he has written over 60 books) and is internationally known for research on the moon and planets.

If I say 'trying to help others on to do things I can't do myself,' it sounds as if I am a do-gooder, which is most certainly not the case. But I don't pretend to have a good academic brain; the one thing I can do is to communicate, either by writing or speaking. This means that quite a number of astronomers, both professional and amateur, have made a start by listening to something I have said, reading something I've written, or looking through my telescope. And this, I suppose, is what I have been trying to do, and what I will continue to do as long as I can.

I do have a few rules, which again are NOT indicative of a do-gooder! They are as follows. When you want to do something, ask yourself three questions. (1) Is it sensible? (2) Will it cause harm to anyone or anything? (3) Will it be useful and/or enjoyable? If the answers are Yes, No and Yes, then do it. If not, don't.

Finally, there are some people who think that life begins and ends on this Earth, and that when our bodies die there is nothing left. If this were true, the universe would be quite pointless. And whatever the universe may be, it is *not* pointless!

Harry Caudill

Harry Caudill as a writer of life and conditions in Appalachia, is a spokesman of the people, the dramatic events and desperate situations that have evolved in the mountain region of eastern Kentucky. A long-time attorney, he is also a former state legislator in Kentucky and a university professor of Appalachian Studies. Caudill is the author of Night Comes to the Cumberlands *and* Slender Is the Thread.

I suppose it is very difficult for anyone to say just what it is that "makes him tick" and keeps him going. In any event, it has to be something outside of and beyond himself. I don't believe that personal gain can be enough to give real meaning to one's life.

I grew up in the Kentucky hills were there is a gray brooding majesty over the land in the winters and where the hills virtually throb with life during the summers. In such an environment one comes to realize that he himself is of little importance. In my case, at least, I came to identify very strongly with the ancient primordial qualities of the land and its life. I was a part of them, but only an insignificant part.

Very early I came to realize that the land shapes people and people shape the land. The two — the land and the people — are intertwined and fall or rise together. They are inseparable. If one is doomed, the other is doomed. Out of this realization I have developed a strong compulsion to preserve the earth, to extend it, to enrich it. I see modern industrial man as an army warring on the sources of his existence. He may well be the greatest geological force since the glaciers crept down over much of the world we now inhabit. With his bombs and his bulldozers, his chemicals and his power plants he may alter the world more drastically than did the glaciers.

With his demonstrated intelligence man should be able to solve all his problems: over-population, energy shortages, environmental pollution, the international tensions that lead to war. To resolve these difficulties we need to act only as reasonable persons on a calm and sustained basis. The lessons I drew from the hills themselves have urged me on to try to persuade others. But these difficulties are not insuperable. Generally, but not always, I receive disbelieving or uncomprehending looks for my efforts.

Sybil Leek

Psychic and author Sybil Leek (1917-1982) was a self-proclaimed witch and believed witchcraft to be a bona fide religion. Leek, who dated her psychic ancestry to the Crusades, lectured on parapsychological phenomena and the occult and wrote a syndicated column and more than sixty books. She was once described as the "Billy Graham of witchcraft."

I have a dedicated acceptance of a Supreme Being which I feel near to in all forces of Nature. I accept the old religion, Wicca, commonly called witchcraft and in following its tenets as faithfully as possible, I find myself in harmony with my environment, with humanity and the sublime force which is within us. I tap into the magic which is within us all and find myself with a great inner peace.

Arnold R. Beisser, M.D.

Forty years ago Arnold Beisser was a doctor. He was a tennis champion and enjoyed an active social life. Then polio struck and he was confined to an iron lung. Since then, in spite of much suffering, Beisser has become a professor of psychiatry in Los Angeles and a respected medical consultant. A courageous and wise man, he is also the author of the successful Flying Without Wings *and the recently published* A Graceful Passage.

Few things are clear, however as a product of the earth and the universe, I am one of its tiny little expressions. As such I contain aspects of both creativeness and destruction, of growth and decline, that I had no conscious part in developing. However, I do have the gift of awareness now, allowing me a choice, at each moment, of which direction to align myself and support. And, by that choice, I believe I will then move the universe a millimicron or so in that direction. I prefer creation and what keeps me going when all seems lost is that I may miss an opportunity.*

*For another answer by Dr. Beisser, see chapter 6.

Thor Heyerdahl

Norwegian archaeologist and writer who captured the hearts of millions around the world when he wrote the bestselling book Kon-Tiki, detailing his adventure in 1947 of sailing a balsa wood raft 4,300 miles from Peru to Polynesia to prove to scientists that Polynesians perhaps were once Peruvians. His books Aku-Aku: The Secret of Easter Island and The Ra Expedition described subsequent expeditions and adventures that also received international attention and admiration.

What makes me tick is the conviction that there is a meaning to this life, and that it has a direct bearing on whatever is to come after. If there was nothing more, the ticking might as well stop today as tomorrow. But why should it stop when it is a scientific fact that time does not exist?

Richard Bolles

Richard Bolles is in a sense a devoted servant to "two" bibles. As an ordained Episcopal minister he serves the Holy Bible. As a writer and counselor he is the author of what has become the career-seeker's bible, What Color Is Your Parachute? Since its first publication in the 1970s, the book has become a publishing phenomenon; it sells about 1,000 copies a day. Bolles says he didn't write the book to make money, which it has. He did it simply to help people, which it has — millions of people.

The Meaning and Purpose of My Life
I think that it is a great gift to be given life, on this earth. I think

there is a Creator, immense, awesomely intelligent, eternally alive, magnificently loving, who gave us this life. The **meaning** of life, for me, is that we came from Him, and to Him we shall go again upon our death. So, I believe the **purpose** of life is to live always, hour by hour, in consciousness of His presence, and in gratitude for this gift. I believe that life should be, and is, both earthy and heavenly, both lusty and spiritual. I have tried and am trying to live such a life, and believe I am the most fortunate man alive to have found a woman, a partner, a soulmate like my wife whom I love deeply, and with whom I can share life's purpose and meaning. I turn to Jesus Christ ever, as my model for life, with keep gratitude to God for having given us such a full reflection of Himself in human form. And I ache for others to know the happiness and fullness I have known in life, despite travails and difficult moments.

A. B. Guthrie, Jr.

*Considered one of the foremost writers on the American West,
A. B. Guthrie is not a "gun and gallop" novelist who celebrates the myth of the West.
Guthrie's best known novels* The Big Sky, The Way West *(1950 Pulitzer Prize winner)
and* These Thousand Hills *realistically depict the people who tamed
the frontier from 1830 to the beginning of the twentieth century.*

What makes me tick, huh?

I could say with some truth, I suppose, it is the felt responsibility to those I love.

But that's not the whole or even the major cause.

I tick out of the inborn or acquired belief that every human being, by the mere fact of being alive, should do his best to justify his occupation of space on the earth. I am not a religious person, but I have the compulsion to account to unknown gods, and I keep trying.

THE FUN OF LIVING IS MYSTERY

*S*ometimes we think we know what makes us keep on: sunlight, bird-song, the sight of children playing. Then a cloud passes over, and we're less sure. To Art Buchwald and other respondents, this uncertainty is what keeps their days lively. The very mystery of life. We don't know exactly who we are with certainty, or if we have a place in the scheme of things. We don't even know when we're going to die. We're a mystery to ourselves and to other people. Only fortuity and providence seem to contain the answers.

When asked the question "What makes you tick?" American physiologist Gustav Eckstein answered by referring to "something that I do not far understand, that seems to race alongside me, and chews at, make of me a slave, a friend, an enemy, a contemporary on the planet in these years." For writer/performer Terry Galloway, the experience of uncertainty is the key with which we open ourselves to art or any creative act.

Perhaps the best strategy is to realize that the mystery in one's life is a good thing and learn to accept it. Otherwise, as William Burroughs warns, if we know too much, "life would be like seeing a film for the second time." Once the outcome is revealed, the challenge of discovery disappears. To these individuals, life is a mystery they haven't finished. They prefer to write the lines and improvise the plot as they go along. And they don't want anyone to tell them the ending. Dee Brown writes, "I suppose it is waiting for the unexpected that keeps most of us going."

There's also this final thought: what one lives for may be uncertain; how one lives is not. Between birth and death, between the world's pleasures and misfortunes, there are two remedies: 1) to enjoy the interval and 2) prepare to live a life of taking chances, of not playing it safe, of being not merely an observer, but a combatant in the arena of action, so that win or lose one comes down on the side of beauty and virtue over ugliness and baseness; that in spite of the uncertainty we strove to elevate the powers of the hyperion in the world and in ourselves and restrict those of the satyr.

Art Buchwald

For over three decades, Art Buchwald has been perhaps the most widely read American political humorist. His worldwide syndicated column (it usually takes him less than an hour to bang out a column) spoofs and satirizes national politics and the muddle of modern life.

I don't know what makes me tick. If I did, I am certain I would not be able to tick. The fun of living is mystery. If you try to figure it all out you may figure it's not worth staying around.

Lowell Thomas

Journalist, explorer, broadcaster, producer, educator, lecturer, editor and author (1892-1981).
A well-known figure to millions of Americans, Lowell Thomas broadcast news on the radio
for nearly a half century. He first gained world recognition as the exclusive biographer of T. E. Lawrence,
whom he was the first to call "Lawrence of Arabia." A well-known world traveler,
Thomas traveled around the world many times in quest of stories.

Some years ago the indomitable Jimmy Doolittle who was our number one national hero sent me a wire. I was in the Ford Hospital at the time, knocked out by too much flying. His comment was: "Lowell, keep up the jet speed but turn off your after-burner."

I've been spinning around this planet nearly all my life, moving so rapidly that I haven't had time to think.

As for the meaning of life, now that I'm approaching my 88th year, I am much interested, and hoping what we call death will simply mean a transfer to some other planet in the cosmos. However, I'm puzzled about this. I wonder if there will be Himalayan peaks to climb, and so on.

So what makes me tick? I spent my youth at an altitude in the Rockies at ten thousand feet. Perhaps this resulted in my acquiring a super something of some sort.

Charles Osgood

CBS news correspondent and the writer and anchor of Newsbreak *and* The Osgood File *on CBS radio. As a TV and radio essayist, Charles Osgood has been called the "Bard of the Airwaves" for the way he can consistently write both humorous verse and thoughtful prose on the day's news.*

It makes me just a little sick
To think about what makes me tick.
Tho all in all I can't complain
About the working of my brain.
I do not think a man can state
What makes his own mind operate,
And that is why I rather doubt
It can be done from inside out.
The only way one can begin
To judge such things is outside in.
The me that others may perceive
Is more objective, I believe.
What makes me tick? I wish I knew.
I'd rather tell you about you.

Luigi Barzini

*Luigi Barzini (1908-1984) was a latter-day Renaissance man.
He was an Italian journalist and foreign correspondent, a member of the Italian Parliment, a philosopher and master of the English language, best known for urbane and often amusing essays and books revealing America to Italians and vice-versa.*

What made me tick? The need not to disgrace my homonymous father, Italy's most famous journalist; the need to make some money; the need to justify my existence on earth; the need to raise another generation of Barzinis in the beliefs which sustained me. Or maybe nothing made me tick. Maybe I was born to do the things I did and couldn't do anything else.

Gustav Eckstein

Gustav Eckstein was a medical doctor, scientist, writer, teacher of physiology and psychiatry and an expert on animal behavior (1890-1981). Capable of writing in many genres, Eckstein was the author of ten books, including the best-selling The Body Has a Head *and a short-lived Broadway play. A biography of Ivan Pavlov was in progress at the time of his death. Eckstein was the model for the character of the ebullient scientist in George S. Kaufman's play* The Man Who Came To Dinner.

The question you ask can be answered, of course, must be answered, by each person singly but I am so driven, and exhausted, by two books I am at (two at a time which is mad) that I just do not have the energy to face that question: What makes me tick? In one sense, the literal sense, it is simply that thing inside my body and I do not mean only the ticking heart, that ticks. In another sense it is not that at all, but rather something that I do not far understand, that seems almost to race alongside me, and chews at me, make of me a slave, a friend, an enemy, a contemporary on the planet in these years.

Russell Baker

One of journalism's wittiest observers of life; his Observer columns (which appear in the New York Times and are syndicated nationally) won the Pulitzer Prize for Distinguished Commentary in 1979. His bestselling autobiography Growing Up *was awarded the Pulitzer Prize in 1983.*

I don't know what makes me tick, but I am now working on a book in which I am trying to work out the answer for myself. If I thought about it very intensely for you and discovered I could summarize it in a paragraph, there would be no more point in writing my own book, and I should probably collapse of acute pointlessness.

Theodor S. Geisel (Dr. Seuss)

World famous writer and illustrator of children's books, including The Cat in the Hat *and* The 500 Hats of Bartholomew Cubbins. *Though he has no children of his own, Theodor Geisel knows what they like to read and has entertained several generations of young readers with his zany nonsense books.*

As much as I respect the sincerity and the purpose of your intended book, I doubt that your readers will learn much that's worthwhile about the people who answer your question, "What makes you tick?"

When you ask a person for a "moment" of his time to answer a "Boswellian Question" you are dealing in a contradiction of terms. In my opinion, you are asking that person to write a meaningful autobiography and then condense it and deep freeze it into a few catch phrases of a TV commercial.

I wish you luck and I hope you succeed. But Mr. Boswell and I have our serious doubts.

Robert Lekachman

Robert Lekachman was a teacher and writer of economics whose maverick views often set him apart from mainstream economists (1920-1989). Lekachman was one of fifty American university instructors selected by Change *magazine in 1986 as having made a significant contribution to undergraduate education. His writings advocated compassion on the part of government toward the underprivileged and reflected his belief that economic growth should coincide with social justice.*

Four years of psychoanalysis failed to make the motives of my actions comprehensible to me. I write and talk as much for any more exalted

56

reason as to discharge assorted anxieties and to reassure myself that I am really alive and, more or less, functioning. I can of course give you a more dignified response which emphasizes my concerns for social justice, diminished inequality, and full employment. These concerns are real, but I doubt that I should have spewed forth the volume of written and spoken comment that I have perpetrated in the absence of severe neurosis.

Elroy Bode

A writer, teacher and student of the Southwest whose sketches and stories perceive the mystery and marvel of existence in such commonplace and ordinary things as trees, twilights, cracks in the sidewalk or walking in a pasture on an autumn day. His books include This Favored Place, Alone in the World Looking *and* To Be Alive.

Your query about *meaning* is a devilishly pertinent and central one to everything I think and do. I have walked more country roads and sat staring into more middle-distances than anyone else I know personally in an effort to come to grips with Meaning. It has dogged me all my adult life, undercutting my tentative efforts at accomplishing things through writing. It has hollowed me out and spurred me on. And now at age 52 I am still no more secure in myself than I was in my twenties: Meaning still eludes me.

I look back, and I can say that I was not bothered with Meaning until I was 17 or so. Up to that point I was basically unreflective. I lived as a child lives—and I was a basically contented child. I *accepted* things: a thing *was* because, well, it *was*.

After 17 the jig was up. I left home, security, church and found myself wide-eyed before Life (Meaning). The universe and a human's place in it, life and death, human values and purposes—the whole incredible business came down on my head and I've been trying to figure out a way to handle it ever since.

Much of the battle of Meaning depends on how much a person accepts more or less ready-made solutions to the Meaning puzzle. Millions of people never seriously question very much about life or human purpose because they accept the answers or rewards of church, family, job, status-seeking, and the like. They are in a cocoon of Meaning, and even when human tragedies and disappointments occur they can handle them because the basic cocoon construction is not threatened.

The search for Meaning drove me to write, and for about twenty years I looked, reflected, and wrote sketches and random pieces. I was an explorer, sending back periodic dispatches about personal discoveries. I assumed, in my innocence, that I would discover Meaning if I just stayed diligent and dogged on my quest. In my early forties I basically gave up the search—and my despair at finding no personal, satisfying answer has caused me to back away from writing.

I remain awed and overwhelmed by the beauties and complexities of the world, and my impulse has been to try to capture, as best as I could, those beauties, those moments of life that touch us deeply...But I have kept bogging down in my Meaning-mire: why bother with one more sketch, one more anything?...I have never satisfactorily answered my own question of my twenties: What is the value of one human life?

Despite the philosophical treatises and the religious dogmas, I don't believe we have a single clue about what's going on in the universe—thus I continue to look out to the afternoon, to the trees, to the silence like the first cave man, waiting for the first rock to speak and break its long silence.

What makes me tick? I don't know—maybe an intensely visual love-affair with the physical world. Maybe sun and trees. Maybe I worship life like a pantheist.

H. B. Fox

Writer of a popular syndicated humor column that appears in many newspapers scattered throughout the United States. The columns are distinguished for their wit, irreverence and folksy political savvy. Fox is author of The 2000-Mile Turtle *and* Dirty Politics Is Fun.

I tick because an ambitious young man migrated from a mountain hollow in Tennessee to Texas, met and married a young piano teacher, and I resulted. I doubt if many people live because of a purpose. They live and work because they're alive and enjoy being that way. I enjoy writing because it's more fun than anything else I can think of. It's fun to be read and get paid for it, but if the chief motivating force isn't the challenge of the writing itself, then one should try some other line of work, like brick-laying or running for Congress. Some have suggested I should have been a bricklayer, but nobody has suggested I run for Congress, an omission I consider a testimony to my good character.

William Burroughs

A leading member of the Beat Generation and a writer of daring literary experiments. The trademark in William Burroughs' writing is his challenge to convention (political, literary, social or sexual). His best known book is Naked Lunch.

It is a rule of life that no one may know what 'makes him tick,' what his real purposes are, though most people think they know and the illusion of knowing is very necessary to them. Occasionally one may glimpse underlying purpose with a shock of surprised recognition. 'Yes that is what I am really doing.' This rule is necessary. Otherwise life would be like seeing a film for the second time.

Morton Mintz

Investigative journalist for the Washington Post *since 1958. Winner of both the Columbia Journalism Award and the A. J. Liebling Award. The focus of much of Morton Mintz's investigative writings is on corporate and governmental abuse of the public trust.*

I apologize for taking so long to reply to your letter of April 12. It has been lying open on my desk ever since it came, and it makes me nervous. I am aware of it when I come into the room, and I feel reproached. The reason is that I do not know the answer to your question but know that I should know it; and I also know that I am not particularly anxious to seek out the answer. "What makes *you* tick?" you ask. "What keeps you going? What is the goal or motive force of your toil?" I have difficulty with the "I" because it presumes a unitary self. I doubt that I have one, and am prepared to believe that, if I do have one, it changes, is highly complex, and embraces contradictions. I honestly don't know, and believe to be unknowable, the exact composition of that which led you to write your letter to me. What weight should be given to reason, intelligence, compassion, generosity of spirit? What role to self-glorification? Ambition? A desire to draw attention to oneself? Meanness? What weight to a professional approach that I may (self-servingly?) think is right? What role to coveting of the esteem (selfishly?) of wife, children, family, friends, peers? I am weighted down by such questions and have, and knew from the outset I wouldn't have, a formulation such as Durant's.

Edward Abbey

Environmentalist, park ranger, fire fighter, educator and writer. Edward Abbey became known as a defender of the world's wilderness areas and a champion of environmental concerns with the publication in 1975 of his book The Monkey Wrench Gang, *which describes an environmentalist group's plan to blow up a dam in Arizona. Author Larry McMurtry called Abbey "the Thoreau of the American West."*

I have no answer to your question. I have no idea why life should exist at all. But it does. Here we are, brothers and sisters. Why not carry it on? Existence is a mystery, but a beautiful mystery.

Nikki Giovanni

Described as the "Princess of Black Poetry," Nikki Giovanni has achieved international prominence as a poet, essayist and lecturer. She was one of the preeminent figures in the 1960s Black literary renaissance and is best known for her books of poems on the themes of self-discovery and Black consciousness.

I don't tick — I live, and in the living we begin to see that life is all about the process. There are no ends separate from the means. I'm simply fasinated by the process.

Henry Steele Commager

One of America's preeminent historians for more than half a century. Through his prolific writings (popular with both scholars and the general reader) he had kindled a love for the spectacle of history and taught people to learn from it.

Alas I cannot help you or respond to your inquiry. I do not know what forces have motivated me throughout my life; I very much doubt that any one really does, and I would regard with suspicion any explanation or rationalization. It is like asking either men or women why they fell in love and married one particular person rather than another. A few might say, for security—and so with careers. Others might give what they suppose to be psychological explanations that are not verifiable. Most, if honest, would say chance, fortuity. Why did I "go into" history rather than law, e.g. Simple answer: I couldn't afford law school—I wrote for my living from the age of 15—and took therefore what now appears to be the easy path. Why American history rather than European?   After all I took my degree in European. Once again, possibly the easiest. One thing is interesting—but I have never been able to explain it: my center of interest has always been the Enlightenment—both in Europe and America...another is my persistent devotion of "liberalism," to Jefferson rather than Hamilton and to FDR rather than Nixon, let us say. The causes of this are forever mysterious.

Terry Gilliam

Terry Gilliam was the lone American member of Monty Python's Flying Circus. Though he rarely appeared in front of the camera, Gilliam was a major force in Monty Python productions. He helped write and also provided all the animation for the British television series; he co-authored and co-directed the Python movies. Gilliam is now co-authoring and directing his own film endeavors, which include Time Bandits, Brazil and The Adventures of Baron Munchausen.

On the simplest level what keeps me going is the feeling that somehow I am useful. On a grander level — I hope the work I do will be good enough to make me worthy of carving my initials on the Tree of Life. But, secretly, what I suspect keeps me going is the simple fact that my internal spring was wound up very tightly before I was born and has managed to unwind at a sufficient rate to keep me ticking away until now...

Terry Galloway

Terry Galloway is a writer and performer from Texas who has won a number of awards. Of her writing, The New York Times said she has helped to create "a new eloquent literature for the deaf." Of her performance, the Los Angeles Times said, "She is sidesplittingly funny."

A sense of uncertainty is my answer. Not the kind that makes for war or catastrophes; not the kind I experienced when I was living in other people's living rooms and eating cream o' wheat three times a day. And not the sense that anything can happen — I hate that feeling; I always interpret it to mean that a black hole could be sucking our galaxy like one long strand of spaghetti into its dark little maw. I find a certain charm in that kind of bleak envisioning; but it always leaves me with a Samuel Johnson like incapacity — periodically he would confine himself to bed and stay there rigid with despair watching the hands of the clock move from hour to hour.

I mean a more sunny kind of uncertainty. The kind of uncertainty that makes for Art or for any creative act. It is, I guess, a certain happy inarticulateness — when I'm uncertain just what it is I've perceived or what effect it is having; but I know that I've perceived something powerful and it is working some kind of change. It makes me feel, not like anything could happen, but that any kind of Art could happen. I like that feeling of uncertainty whether I'm creating or just beholding.

Dee Brown

Novelist and historian Dee Brown has written many nonfiction books and novels about the early American West. His books have dealt with such subjects as the building of the railroads, the massacre at Little Big Horn, and pioneer women settlers. However, his most famous book, the bestselling Bury My Heart At Wounded Knee *(1970), forced us to see the settling of the American West in the nineteenth century in a totally new light — from the Indian's perspective. Vividly describing the wholesale destruction of the American Indian's ancient civilization,* Bury My Heart At Wounded Knee *buries the myth that the white conquest of the West was civilization's mission or manifest destiny. In this and other works, Brown writes about Indians with compassion and understanding.*

I have pondered the question you ask — why I do the things I do — but the answer is no more clear to me now that it was fifty years. To me life is totally meaningless and unpredictable, yet is filled with delightful suspense and surprising wonders. I suppose it is waiting for the unexpected that keeps most of us going.

I can no more answer your question than I can tell you the meaning of Ozymandias or the answer to the riddle of the Sphinx.

ONE THOUSAND HOURS OF SUFFERING AND ONE HOUR OF BLISS

*W*hat is it that can make us endure so much for so little? For these correspondents the answer is an enthusiasm for an object whose value grows in proportion to its spirituality — such as a passion for music, or the joy that comes from writing a poem, or the effort to preserve memories from the rush of time. And inevitably, the moment of consummation is brief compared to the long labor that made it possible. Word-obsessed Larry Gelbart writes, "Being a wordaholic is to be in a constant state of metaphoria, engaged in a ceaseless search for clarification."

It's interesting, but not surprising, that none of the writers claim money, fame, pleasure or material goods as their prime motivators. None suggest these things are irrelevant; it's just that they are a little like star football players in high school, receiving attention disproportionate to their real worth. They can compel envy and effort, but not suffering. Bliss comes from a struggle for the good life, not the goods life. As Molly Ivins writes, "I hope to have as my epitaph: She Never Made a Shrewd Career Move."

And for some people, the suffering and work is as much a part of the process as the reward. As philosopher Brand Blanshard noted, a key to effective ticking is to create a marriage between one's work and play, so that in the end one can look back and say, "Yes, it was a lot of toil and work, but, damn, it was fun."

Antonia Brico

Conductor; pianist; lifelong struggler against sex discrimination in the orchestral world (1902-1989). Antonia Brico, who was the subject of the 1974 film Antonia: Portrait of a Conductor, *managed to break many barriers in the male-dominated music world. She lived in Denver, Colorado, where she taught music and directed the Denver Community Symphony and the Denver Opera.*

My passion for music is so enormous that were it not for that, I would have cracked up long ago, because of the many difficulties as a "woman conductor." Music is a very beautiful influence. My secretary asked someone one day, someone who had know me in my Berlin study years in the late '20s, if she noticed that I loved music then, and this friend said, "She didn't love music, she was obsessed by it."

In answer to your questions as to what makes me "tick," when one is so passionately devoted to something, it gives you the strength to overcome all sorts of odds and difficulties, of which I had plenty. I love music and conducting beyond the telling, and I have said many times, one thousand hours of suffering and one hour of bliss, and it is worth it.

Carlos Montoya

Carlos Montoya is a Spanish-born guitarist who is America's leading purveyor of Spanish flamenco music. Carlos Montoya was the first to champion flamenco guitar as a solo art in the mid-1940s. In his eighties now, he still performs concerts all over the world. When he travels, he buys an extra plane ticket for his guitar; so the hand-made instrument never sees the inside of a baggage compartment.

I am writing for my husband because my husband's English is inadequate to answer your questions. I will try to explain what he believes, although he is a strictly intuitive person, not intellectual. Maybe you don't know that Flamenco music is unwritten, with a great deal of improvisation. It exactly expresses his attitude towards life.

To begin with, he was born with a great gift. He has told me many times that when he was young he always felt that he could do something in life with the guitar. His mother died before he was 15, but she always said, My Carlos will be "somebody." He attributes his success to his perseverance in continuing his efforts to make a name for himself on the guitar. He wanted to make his way by his own efforts, as he was and is a "free spirit." No one can tell a gypsy what to do.

He started playing at age 8 and working professionally from 14 on. The proof of the drive he had, whatever its motivation, is that now, at age 76, he still tours and plays with the same enthusiasm.

— Sally Montoya

Edwin Way Teale

Considered by many to have been one of the most knowledgeable and far-traveled naturalists in America, Edwin Way Teale (1899-1980) introduced many readers to wildlife and nature through his photograpahs and text. His Wandering Through Winter *(1966) won the Pulitzer Prize.*

I think I can best explain what has kept me working beyond the age of eighty, after having had more than thirty books published, by quoting some paragraphs from the books...

(Ever since I was a boy I have been keeping journals of my experiences out-of-doors, trying to preserve what gave me delight from the all-consuming rush of time, trying to keep them intact—like insects preserved in amber—to be enjoyed again and again. My books have recorded that part of our lives we would gladly live again. They are personal, almost like private journals, written, in the first place, mainly for ourselves, to "catch from fleeting time" things we want to remember always.)

"Mine, I realize, is an emotional as well as a visual memory. It is often concerned with moods and atmospheres, scenes and appearances, shifting tints and fragrances, lights and shadings. Even when I was very small I remember standing entranced as a sunset altered minute by minute. At the time I felt: I want to remember this always. I want to be able to recall this *very* sunset just as it is now whenever I desire to see it again.

70

Even in those early years, I was acutely aware of how time is ceaselessly sliding away, streaming to the rear, carrying with it moments that have affected me deeply. Always I have wanted to salvage such moments from the rush of time, to preserve them permanently in memory, to enjoy them again and again in retrospect. I have been a lifelong hoarder of memories." (*A Walk Through the Year*)

"I return home at the close of this day of onrushing spring wishing I could experience it all over, know it again on a thousand days, see the same scene unchanged, hear the same birds sing, stand among the same wildflowers just as I stood today. But I know that this can never be. But it is something to have the memory set down in a journal, to have it preserved on a printed page. In nature, everything flows. All is change. In truth, we never cross the same river twice. But the printed page does not change. It is the river we can cross again." (*A Walk Through the Year*)

The effort to achieve this comes the closest to explaining what "makes me tick," why I have worked so hard to achieve this personal end for so many years.

Robert Nisbet

Although he is a sociologist by profession, most of Robert Nisbet's writing have explored areas where sociology, intellectual history, philosophy and political science intersect. As the title of one of his popular books indicates (History of the Idea of Progess), Nisbet is a historian of ideas.

I was not born with genius or relentless desire for work. But I did receive from the gods a substantial amount of sheer good luck, all or most of it having to do with books. From my mother and father I acquired very early a respect for, then a virtual passion for books. From age 5 on, I read as constantly as school and the necessity for job permitted. For a great many years all I wanted was the time to read and read and read—books in nearly all spheres, fiction highup, except mathematics and the natural sciences. The next piece of luck was being put in very close relationship with two or three professors at the

71

University of California, Berkeley who, on all counts, became role-models, so to speak, in my life, and inasmuch as they wrote books, books that I admired, the desire to write began to be an ineradicable part of my essence. Again I was lucky. The first manuscript I sent off to publishers—in 1948—was a bad one and was properly recognized as such and turned down. That stung me enough to settle down to real work on a book, and as the result my first one, *The Quest for Community*, came out, a moderate success, in 1953. Then luck failed me, for I found an offer to go into academic-administrative work irresistible. Ten years of near-sterility followed. But then my luck returned, and I mustered up the resolve to get out of administration, at considerable sacrifice of income, and return to the writing of books. With one or two exceptions, all have been successful: not financially, but in the terms of reader-response. I am now officially retired, but I shall continue writing until disease or death stops me. I wish I could say that what makes me tick is Aristotelian or Leibnizian passion for knowledge, but I can't. What makes me tick, as I reflect on it, is, much more simply, passion for books. I enjoyed seeing my twelfth book come off the press the other day just as much as I did my first, twenty-seven years ago. I hope I may see my twentieth.

Archibald MacLeish

American poet and three-time Pulitzer Prize winner for his poems and the play J.B. Known primarily as a man of words, Archibald MacLeish (1892-1982) was also a man involved in public affairs —Assistant Secretary of State (1944-45), Librarian of Congress (1939-44).His poetry rejected the isolation of an ivory tower and concerned itself with all aspects of life.

It is a good question. In fact it is, or should be the question to which we devote our life. And our work is the answer—*all* our work. There is no way to paraphrase or condense, which is why we read Shakespeare —*all* of Shakespeare. All of Dante. All of Donne.

John Ciardi

To millions of Americans, John Ciardi (1916-1986) was Mr. Poet, the one who wrote
(25 published volumes), talked, taught, edited, translated, criticized and propelled poetry
into a popular, lively art. In his later years, a love of words and interest in etymology led him
to compile the multi-volume A Browser's Dictionary.

As long as you don't insist on beard-stroking profundity...

You've said it yourself: we *demand* purpose. The fact that it may not exist is no obstacle. We still demand it. Having gone to the trouble of inventing Him, we demand God, we demand that he remember our names, and that he set up housekeeping for us in eternity. We get these imperatives, I suspect with mother's milk, which is not only delicious but hallucinogenic. With it we suck both love and nonsense and then spend the rest of our lives confusing the two.

Nonsense aside, existence is an animal surge, an energy sexpending itself because that is what the energy is for. When I was younger I wanted all the pretty girls there were for the excellent reason that they were there and I was able. I suppose that impulse might reasonably have made me a rapist, but I had in fact been infected by love and it was never my pleasure to be brutal. I am not a rapist today because I cannot pass the physical.

I do what I find I am able to do. Words have become my habit in about the way nuts are a squirrel habit. I still have a basically affectionate nature, but I also don't care to be bothered by fools. I don't attack fools: like a squirrel I try to go inconspicuously up my tree and out of their way. I keep storing because storage occupies me. Sometimes, having fed on my hoard, I race about in my psychic tree for the joy of the jumping and running, and to test my balance, but I have no hope of being as graceful at it as are the squirrels in my (actually surviving and flourishing) elm. I am glad they are there for me to watch. They and the universe. I don't demand anything of either squirrels or universes but insist on my right to watch and to take pleasure from them.

I couldn't say this unless I had found life good. I recognize that it can become unbearable: I watched my mother take years to die painfully and lacked the courage to kill her mercifully, but I think, should my own

life become unbearable (as, say, in a terminal cancer), I will be able to
sit down with 50 barbituates and a bottle of good bourbon and offer a
reasoned resignation.

I don't demand. From who should I demand? I am having an experience. I do what I do because I find pleasure in doing it — even in
answering your demands.

But why ask me? Our Sun is a better witness. At some more or less
known point in its evolutionary cycle, it will flare up into a nova, sub-
limating everything in the solar system, and at that point there will be
no brain cell left to demand purpose — and QED eternity.

There remains this meanwhile. Had we not been hallucinated into
demanding things from an ego-centric universe, we might have made
a happier species, and almost certainly a less bloody one. I go on trying
to match systole to diastole about one to one, and I keep discovering
how I feel about it, and when I can I try to make poems out of what
comes because the act of trying to make a poem is joyously consuming.
Now and then the process even permits me the illusion that I have found
an acorn. To squirrel man, an acorn is something to live by, a good of
its own. I can't totally stop my hallucination, but I can at least tell it to
shut up till I have finished eating.

Brand Blanshard

*A philosopher, writer and elegant stylist of over 300 books and articles; and Sterling Professor Emeritus
of Philosophy at Yale University. Brand Blanshard (1892-1987) was known as a rationalist, a believer
in the intelligibility of the world and its accessibility to reason. An immensely popular lecturer at Yale
University, Blanshard received a standing ovation at the end of each lecture in his last semester.*

In a letter of many weeks ago (my apologies) you ask what makes
me tick. The answer is: two things.

(1) In my sophomore year in college I fell in love with philosophy.
My father had been a minister; I took it almost for granted that I should
follow in his track; and I conceived of philosophy as the doughtiest
weapon with which to rout the unbelievers. I came with the years to

see that philosophy is no one's servant, and that its business is to follow the argument, whereever it leads. In my case it led me to abandon most of the belief in which I had been brought up. But the process of reflective inquiry has become a lifelong vocation which has given me endless satisfaction. It need not cease with age; much of my better work has been done after retirement...I am now eighty-eight years old, and am half way through a new book.   My special field of interest is reason and reasonableness, both in theory and in practice; and I feel sure that the attempt to live up to my own conclusions has been a prolific source of such happiness and serenity as I have enjoyed.

(2) Early in life I acquired an interest in style. It came indirectly through an interest in debating and public speaking. I learned that to write effectively one must hear what one writes; writing that lacks rhythm is almost a physical pain to me. But the result has been that the manner in which my books have been written has cost me almost as much effort as what I have said. The pleasure of trying to write well, like the pleasure of thinking itself, is one that lasts and increases.

One of the secrets of a smoothly ticking life is to find work that one enjoys. For forty years I was a college and university teacher. I always took pleasure in teaching, so in some ways my life has been an idyllic one. Satisfaction in one's work is largely a function of doing it well, and I think people should study the technique of their work, whether it lies in cleaning a house or electric wiring or repairing cars; for the rightly adjusted man or woman, there is no sharp line between work and play.

John Bowle

Distinguished British historian (1905-1985) who excelled at narrative history and biography. Bowle succeeded in bringing a scene to life with an exceptional eye for its color and peculiarities. He is the author of many books, including Man Through the Ages, From the Origins to the Eighteenth Century *and* Minos or Minotaur? The Dilemma of Political Power.

What Keeps Me Going
I have always since childhood been fascinated by history and have

75

never doubted what I wanted to do. Like ordinary travel, time travel enriches the mind, and I have always wanted to recreate the past. This impulse is bound up with my strong feeling for place and character and with my ability to draw and paint, also apparent since childhood. Much of my writing attempts to create pictures of the past as well as to recreate the characters of my subject — as Henry VIII and Charles I. Why the people in history are more interesting to me than are most of my contemporaries I do not know why: but they always have been. In a sense my impulse is romantic — an attempt to escape from the conflicting and uncongenial aspects of modern mechanized civilization, which goes along with my preference for country life over metropolitan existence. My main talent is to write, narrate, and teach; but I am incapable of even elementary mathematics and though I respect science, I cannot practice it...

Apart from my narrative history and biography and political theory, I have drawn pleasure and inspiration from pictures and sculptures which often reflect more closely the civilization that produced them than that other more ephemeral aspect. You will see from these observations that my work as an historian through writing, teaching, and discussion have been central to my life, and helpful to make me "tick" by giving me a permanent objective. This objective has been decided for me by my cast of mind, my talent, and my limitations in the more abstract fields. But it has given me increasing satisfaction through my life.

Sir Alec Guinness

British actor and international star of theatre and film, Guinness is famed for his versatility and admired as an actor who makes one forget that he is acting. That quality is made memorable in his performances on stage ("The Cocktail Party", "Dylan", "A Walk in the Woods"), on film ("The Man in the White Suit", "The Bridge on the River Kwai", "Tunes of Glory"), and on TV ("Tinker, Tailor, Soldier, Spy").

I can't answer your letter satisfactorily. Where I detect motives in my life I consider them very personal and private. I am not aware of "ticking" —which always sounds to me like mechanical ambitions.   When I work at what I like I feel alive—when not working dull. It's as simple as that.

William Manchester

Historian, journalist, writer and teacher. William Manchester attributes his popularity as a writer to his narrative style rather than his controversial approach. "The goal of all my books is to re-create the past, to make the reader feel it, smell it," Manchester said. Praised and criticized by critics, many of Manchester's works focus on power and its use and abuse. His books include The Death of a President *(he was the designated historian by Mrs. John F. Kennedy of President Kennedy's death);* The Arms of Krupp, The Glory and the Dream, American Caesar *(a biography of General Douglas MacArthur) and* The Last Lion *(a two-volume biography of Winston Churchill).*

I try, each day, to expiate yesterday's guilt.

Larry Gelbart

Larry Gelbart is a writer of comedy and was the principal writer for the first four seasons of "M*A*S*H" on television. He is best known for writing very funny scripts which have been known to make people laugh and cry at once. His City of Angels *won the Tony Award for best book of a muscial on Broadway in 1990. He was a co-author of the Tony Award winner* A Funny Thing Happened on the Way to the Forum, *and received Oscar nominations for* Oh, God *in 1977 and* Tootsie *in 1982, a movie he co-wrote.*

Words make me tick. In my case, words are, in fact, a tic — the manipulation and management of them is an endless, involuntary, exhausting process. Often times, a single word; sometimes, two; other times, a group of them, traveling together as a thought; one way or another, they are forever appearing on the monitor of my mind. Being a wordaholic is to be in a constant state of metaphoria, engaged in a ceaseless search for clarification. The meaning of my life is beyond me. The best I can do is deal with it one word at a time.

Molly Ivins

Molly Ivins is a political columnist for the Dallas Times-Herald who writes about Texas and national politics. Honest, amusing, irreverent, insightful and never boring, Ivins is also a contributing writer to many national publications. In addition, she has done guest essays for the "MacNeil/Lehrer Report" and National Public Radio's "All Things Considered."

I have a real dislike of bumpersticker philosophy — seems to me invariably trite and shallow. Nevertheless, I'll take a stab at it. I believe in Doing Good, Having Fun and Learning. I hope to have as my epitaph: She Never Made A Shrewd Career Move.

THE CENTER OF MY LIFE HAS
ALWAYS BEEN THE LOVE I HAVE
BEEN GIVEN BY OTHERS

*T*here is a "New Yorker" cartoon that shows a flat, desolate, treeless landscape littered with only a rubber tire, an empty bottle and tin can, and some scattered rocks. In the background is a foreboding dark sky. The caption reads "LIFE WITHOUT MOZART."

These letters make the same point, except they substitute the word "LOVE" for "MOZART"— the love of nature and art and great photography, the love given to us by others, and, as Eugene Kennedy writes, the love expressed in "giving one's self away in love, despite the constant presence of separation and death."   Dr. Bernard Siegel believes love is the greatest healer. He says he's seen people grow up feeling they were unloveable and they "live in pain and turn out to be Hitlers."

We need our daily bread, and we need our daily measure of self-development, but we also need more importantly daily love. We are irredeemably connected with one another, and without love's presence our lives will resemble the deserted landscape in the cartoon — and that is nothing to laugh about.

Sir Kenneth M. Clark

Kenneth M. Clark (1903-1983) enjoyed a varied career as a eminent art historian, director of the National Gallery in London, educator and author. He is perhaps most widely remembered as the creator of "Civilization," the highly successful thirteen-part British television series in which he presented personal commentary on Western culture of the past thirteen hundred years.

> What makes me tick?
> LOVE,
> of nature, of art, of music,
> of poetry and of
> individuals.

Eugene Kennedy, Ph.D.

Noted lecturer, prolific writer, professor of psychology at Loyola University of Chicago and acclaimed novelist. As a priest he has written widely on the Catholic Church. Theologian David Tracy described him as "our best critic of American Catholic life and thought."

I am reminded by your request of what Picasso said when someone asked him what he was doing when he was created. His response was: "Don't talk to the driver."

Such an answer must be given to the question of what makes one tick, because the price of ticking in any constructive and profitable way is a lack of self-consciousness. I think I ride the tides of my geneology and social inheritance and I have found no fancy names for these except that I am Irish and Catholic and that I am living out again the same dreams that have been common to all those who have shared the same culture.

One must recognize that one is part of a larger human story in which the vital things have always been the same. They have always centered on the great journey of finding one's self by giving one's self away in love and life, despite the constant presence of separation and death, following the bidding of what is deepest and truest in our human struggle, to survive and to do better for the next generation. But nobody goes so far if he or she thinks too much about these times or if he or she thinks one has to conduct a field expedition to derive meaning. The great thing is to respond without worrying about how you move or whether you are doing it the right way.

I am blessed by being curious, energetic, and charmed by everything human. The center of my life has always been the love I have been given by others—my family, my wife, and those with whom I work. A man who has these things does not have to search far for meaning to have an understanding of the source of the energies that keep him going.

C. Northcote Parkinson

*British historian, novelist, and satirist of managerial bureaucracy in government and business.
C. Northcote Parkinson is probably best known for his creation of "Parkinson's Law," which states that
"Work expands to fill the time available for its completion."*

The motive power and direction of my efforts has derived from three sources. First, I knew that my parents had done much to further my career and I felt bound to justify their efforts. I had to succeed in something. My father had been a penniless orphan who made himself a scholar, a gentleman, and active head of a school. My mother was a musician and occasional authoress. They made many sacrifices to give me an education. I gained much from their support, more from their example. Second, I inherited from them and learnt from them a love of beauty in every form, artistic, literary, musical, and dramatic. Given power or wealth I should want, above all, to create beauty and order. I should want to leave behind me a legacy of architecture gardens, plays, films and art. Third, I developed for myself a number of intellectual ideas, some at least partly original, covering a wide range of subjects, whether historical, literary, political, warlike or administrative.

84

Of these three sources the first two have been more important, the one providing momentum, the other providing intended direction. The third seems to me more accidental, more affected by experience, more influenced by other people. I have been thwarted or deflected by my own limitations, by the society in which I live, by the age in which I chance to have been born. I could easily have been an artist, a lawyer, a producer, a headmaster or soldier. What position I have gained is the result of obstacles encountered and opportunities which have offered. My career may well have been hindered by my versatility, my too ready response to any challenge. This was, however, an inherited versatility and probably inescapable. Over the age of seventy now, I look back on many failures, a few achievements, some good fortune and some ill luck, but I feel, when nearing the end of my career, that I probably did the best with what I had.

Freeman Dyson

Freeman Dyson is a scientist whose professional interests include mathematics, nuclear physics, rocket technology and astrophysics; and whose personal interests range from social and political issues to music and literature He is very concerned with the long-range moral and social fallout of today's scientific miracles. Dyson is the author of Disturbing the Universe *and* Weapons and Hope.

The bird a nest,
The spider a web,
Man friendship.
  (William Blake, 1793)

Andrew M. Greeley

Andrew Greeley is not your average Catholic priest. Since he was ordained in 1954, Greeley has become a sociologist, teacher, a weekly columnist, one of the nation's leading authorities on the sociology of religion, an outspoken critic of the official conservative trends in Catholicism, author of countless *nonfiction works on religion, and a novelist of numerous bestselling novels. Greeley is very generous with the money from his books: he has given $1 million to inner-city Chicago schools and $1.5 million to the University of Chicago.*

I work, I suppose, because I believe I am caught up in an exciting adventure; a romance, a love affair, a comedy. I'm afraid if I slowed down and stopped working, I would miss the jokes and the laughter that comedy provides.

Arnold R. Beisser, M.D.

Forty years ago Arnold Beisser was a doctor. He was a tennis champion and enjoyed an active social life. Then polio struck and he was confined to an iron lung. Since then, in spite of much suffering, Beisser has become a professor of psychiatry in Los Angeles and a respected medical consultant. A courageous and wise man, he is also the author of the successful Flying Without Wings *and the recently published* A Graceful Passage.

Few things are clear and they change continuously. I need a reason for getting out of bed in the morning . . . people and things I love, my wife, a friend, a patient or something I want to write. Without them my life would seem unbearable and meaningless. Many times in the past I have lost who or what I loved, so saw no hope. I am not fickle, yet eventually to my surprise, I developed new loves and new meanings. It is harder now, as I grow older and at some point it may be too hard, but evidently I am more adaptable than I expect.*

*For another answer by Dr. Beisser, see chapter 3, page 46.

Bernie Siegel, M.D.

A pediatric and general surgeon, a recognized authority in the field of advanced cancer and a teacher at Yale University Medical School. Dr. Bernie Siegel's book Love, Medicine, and Miracles *(1986) became a best-seller. In it he advocates engaging patients to become participants in healing. Siegel is now involved in humanizing medical education and making the medical profession aware of the mind-body connection. His beliefs have sparked a polite medical controversy.*

What keeps me going is the knowledge that the world was created to express love and as an expression of love.

Yet because it takes free will to make the love meaningful so much can and does go wrong.

I see people who grow up feeling they were unloveable from the moment of birth. People who live in pain and turn out to be Hitlers.

This knowledge and experience keeps me going in the hope that I can help some of them find self love by loving them and showing them they are loveable.

In simple terms I want to heal my life and help others heal theirs and love is the greatest healer.

If every child is loved, the planet is healed and survives too.

Mary Ellen Mark

Award-winning photojournalist and one of the few photojournalists whose gripping pictures have regularly appeared in Life, The Sunday Times of London, The New York Times Magazine, Rolling Stone, Paris-Match, Stern, *and* Time. *Much of her work reflects a deep social passion and empathy for women and people on the fringes of society, such as the starving in Ethiopia, the homeless, immigrant residents in Austrialia, adolescent runaways and teenage heroin addicts.*

WHAT MAKES ME TICK
1. A curiosity and love of people — mostly the unknown and "unfa-mous" who live on the edges of society and who have not had the

lucky breaks in life.
2. I am a perfectionist and I have an almost compulsive drive to learn more about my craft. I want to continue to grow as an artist. I want to get better and better.
3. I have a great respect for integrity.
4. I have a wonderful husband whom I love. He is my best friend and he inspires me and encourages me in my work.
5. A love for great photography.

SOME INGREDIENTS IN THE STEW
WOULD BE

Some people see man as basically an animal, others see him as a biologically driven machine. Poet Howard Neverov sees his life as a stew made up of varied ingredients, an analogy I like because it recognizes that many factors make each individual tick, just as many different ingredients are required to make a stew — a fact which I doubt an animal or machine knows anything about.

Principal (but often ignored) among these "ingredients" are the spices and condiments that give flavor to the recipe of day-to-day living. It seems that so much of our time and energies are spent in making a living or getting a meal on the table that little time is left over to just enjoy living or make a life. Too often, we confuse the demands of survival and success with the needs of fulfillment and wind up in a state of material affluence but spiritual squalor. The throw-ins of condiments and spices — reveling in the change in the seasons, or listening to favorite music, or knowing the satisfaction of a task well done — are the flavorful secret to a well-lived life or a successful stew.

Archibald Cox

*A leading authority on constitutional and labor law and a noted professor of law, Archibald Cox
is probably best known as the first Watergate Special Prosecutor (1973).
Now, he is chairman of the citizens' lobbying group Common Cause.
During the Truman Administration Cox served as chairman of the
Wage Stabilization Board and from 1961 to 1965 was Solicitor General of the U.S.*

How does one summarize his philosophy of life without sounding
—perhaps being—pompous?

One force is surely the satisfaction of using to the fullest such talents
and energies as we were given.

Next is the sense of being part of a great, on-going human adventure
with a past and a future — a sense which leads one to aspire to leave
the world just a little better than he found it.

And, surely, for the lucky — and I have been lucky — another source
of motivation is that a full life is fun.

Marquis W. Childs

*Veteran journalist on the Washington staff of the St. Louis Post Dispatch for over 30 years.
Childs (1903-1990) won a Pulitzer Prize in 1969 for political commentary.*

I hope that what I have to say may be useful to you. I am writing
in the odd half hour left of the day. First, may I ask you not to use that
expression, What makes you tick? It is too tired a cliche´. I like motive
force.

I am somewhat at a loss to answer. I was interested in journalism
at a very early age; the desire I suppose to know what makes events
happen. And that has been a continuing motivation over a period of
many years. It is probably the motive that leads me to go writing the

93

column when it might have been wise to have put it down some time ago. But let me add that personal ambition has certainly been a motivating force; the desire to be listened to, to be known, to talk with the world's leaders as I have. It is difficult to separate these motives. I have had a lot of fun on the way and this may have been a motive—to see and to laugh at the follies of mankind. This may sound too cynical but it has been matched by a strong current of idealism, the hope that the world may be a better place and that in some small way I might contribute to its betterment. The last, I'm afraid, is a lost hope.

Malcolm Boyd

Gay Episcopal clergyman, civil rights activist, anti-Vietnam War protester, and "expresso priest" who attracted national attention when he moved religion into coffeehouses during the 1960s and read from his popular avant-garde book of prayers, Are You Running With Me, Jesus?

I tick strongly, and often I've wondered why. I guess it's because meaning is absolutely necessary for me. I cannot (and do not) exist without it. I refuse to be a vegetable, an object (to be used or manipulated), a 'thing.'

Indeed, I find something approaching absolute meaning—this, amid the paradoxes and ambiguities with which I must coexist. Yet there is a purpose always; so, life becomes a journey towards a destination, even a pilgrimage.

What keeps me going? Meaning—and hope, and (yes) love. If not love before my very eyes, at least the search for it—in, as well as outside, myself.

The goal or motive of my toil is synthesis—perspective—understanding—the 'center'—illumination—finally/immediately: not through a glass darkly, but face to face.

I feel an incredible flow of energy in the fact of life. I accept, and honor, and use, and passionately engage myself with this energy.

Howard Nemerov

United States Poet Laureate, Library of Congress (1988).
Howard Nemerov is a highly acclaimed poet whose poems relate a broad spectrum of emotion
and a variety of concerns. A distinguished professor at Washington University in St. Louis since 1969,
Nemerov's books have earned him every major award for poetry, including the National Book Award, the
Pulitzer Prize, the Bollingen Prize and the National Medal of Art.

There is no single answer to your question, and if there were I should think it bad luck to know it. None of us knows why he is whatever he is; indeed, it is very uncertain that any of us knows *that* he is whatever he is.

Some ingredients in the stew would be: good health, lately a little flawed by arthritis; a good wife, fine children, a domestic life in the main tranquil and good-natured; a few shabby vestiges of military discipline remaining from the War; and a vast self-indulgence especially in such matters as booze and cigarettes.

Of course, none of this catalogue of virtues and fortunes could prevent The Book of Job from starting tomorrow if it pleased the Creator and his buddy Satan.

Charles Alan Wright

Noted professor of law at the University of Texas School of Law.
Recognized in the legal field as an authority on American constitutional law and matters of the
Federal courts and their rules and procedures.

I share Mr. Durant's uncertainty about whether I "tick," and I am not even sure what the word means. But if you are asking what purpose it is that motivates me, I think there are two answers.

First is the mere satisfaction of doing something and knowing that it is done well. I suspect that a good cook derives the same satisfaction when he or she takes the finished dish out of the oven and knows that something good has been produced. Compliments later from those who eat it may be nice, but they are less important than the feeling that I have done what I have set out to do and I have done it well.

The other is the opportunity to influence people and events. It is very satisfying to think that someone is now a better person or a better lawyer because of what I have given them either by precept or example in the classroom. It is very satisfying to argue a difficult case before the United States Supreme Court and to win it so that the Constitution is construed in the fashion that I think proper. It is very satisfying to read the opinions of courts and to see how often they turn to my books for guidance on what the law is and accept my views on what the law ought to be.

Albert Ellis, Ph.D.

Clinical psychologist, marriage counselor, writer and originator of the Rational-Emotive Psychotherapy Movement, which rejects Freudian theories and advocates the belief that emotions come form conscious thought "as well as internalized ideas of which the individual may be unaware."

What Makes Me Tick

Many things make me tick and give me real zest to face each day, in spite of my age (67) my physical ailments (diabetes, easily tired eyes, frail body), a fairly crummy decade so far (inflation, energy shortages, terrorism, mugging, wars, and what you will), and life's inevitable limitations (a paltry 24 hours in each day in a miserably short—93 years, I hope, like my mother lived)—life span. Some of those things? Well—

Determination to discover—what things are about; what makes living creatures tick.

Determination to solve—world problems; efficiency problems; human problems.

Determination to hear—many kinds of music, particularly symphonic and light classical.

Determination to propagate my ideas—particularly, today, those basic to rational-emotive therapy (RET), which I disseminate, just about 365 days every year, to individual and group therapy clients; by public and professional talks and workshops; through radio and TV presentations; and by voluminous writings.

Determination to engage in sex-love relationships—old ones to be maintained and revivified; new ones to be made—or at least dreamed about! Most of all, what makes me tick at present involves two pursuits:

Determination to discover what makes people tick—how their emotional blocks can be removed and how they can lead happier, less disturbed lives.

Determination to personally use my discoveries about people—so that I can continue, as I have done for many years, to stubbornly refuse to be utterly miserable about practically anything!

Harvey Cox

One of American Protestanism's most influential theologians, Harvey Cox is a professor of Divinity at Harvard Divinity School and author of many books on religion and ethics. Through his books (The Secular City, Religion in the Secular City) Cox has sought to develop a secular-political theology to bring Christianity into a more meaningful relationship with man and his problems in modern technological soceity.

A certain love for the species of human beings—especially as represented by those closest to me: this plus a faith that Providence still brings strangely positive things out of grotesque and ugly ones — all this keeps me going. Plus music, the change of seasons, the message of and about Jesus.

Edward James Olmos

The star of such films as Stand and Deliver *and* The Ballad of Gregorio Cortez, *and the man who played Lieut. Castillo on television's "Miami Vice" is an award-winning, leading Hispanic-American actor of his generation. He also works to try to alleviate present problems of society. He visits hospitals, schools, Indian reservations, detention centers, speaking up for education and against drugs.*
A serious and consumate actor, Olmos seeks in his work to make people aware of the common humanity and differences that exist in our intercultural relationships.

Being grateful and thankful with each waking day. No matter what comes...I enjoy greeting it, than not!

Patience, Determination, Perseverance and the Key...Discipline...

My Goal is to be the oldest living Olmos to date...I will die trying...

FIGHT FOR THE HIGHEST
ATTAINABLE AIM

We all yearn to succeed in what we do, but for these individuals, the only success worth striving for is the highest attainable aim, such as giving one's life in the service of the poor, or cracking the riddle of cancer, or fighting against the persistence of ignorance and self-deception in oneself and others.

Of course, to talk about what makes one tick is tantamount to talking about what makes one happy. And here, the respondents force us to rethink the definition of happiness. Popularly conceived, happiness is looked upon as a sundial, recording only the sunny hours in the day, only its pleasures and comforts. However, a new definition is emerging that emphasizes the intensity of living over complete satisfaction or satiety: which says that it's better to fail building castles in the air or be pained and troubled in a good cause than settle for a long easy coast to extinction, engaged in only shallow pursuits — happy as a clam.

Nor should we narrow our scope to only one aim. As Jacques Barzun and other correspondents remind us, a person's goals and aims can vary with time, mood, and circumstance. In his early days, Walter Sullivan tells us he wanted to be a music critic. Today, however, he seeks to extend scientific knowledge.

Each man in this time, says Shakespeare, plays many roles. The message of these letters is that there are really several people lying within each person, nestling inside one another like wooden Russian dolls: each demanding to be opened, each containing angels and demons waiting to be reckoned with. The tragedy for many people is that the boxes will remain closed, like clams that will never open.

Denton A. Cooley, M.D.

One of the world's greatest heart surgeons, Denton Cooley is a leader and pioneer in the field of cardio-vascular surgery. He has been particularly active in combating congenital heart diseases in infants.

My primary motivation in continuing my program of hard work and dedication stems from a longheld desire to excel at anything I undertake. I enjoy activity. I like to set high and almost unattainable goals. I am a firm believer that hard work is the most reliable means to attain one's goals.

Fortunately, I have chosen a profession which suits me well. The opportunities for work in cardiovascular surgery is unlimited. The grat-ification which one derives from the healing arts is unequaled in any other profession. The challenges in cardiac and vascular surgery are even greater since the field is a relatively new one of the past few decades. Therefore, those of us involved in this profession and speciality are priv-iliged to be pioneers, explorers and creators.

Norman Cousins

Since recovering from a rare collagen disease (described in his bestseller Anatomy of an Illness), *Norman Cousins, longtime editor of* The Saturday Review, *has become a professor of medical humanities at UCLA where he explores the interaction of emotions with disease and healing.*

You are asking, essentially, about my basic drives. My motivations and goals tend to coincide:

1) The need to work for sanity and responsibility in the actions and interactions of nations;

2) The need to persuade human beings that they are the most priv-ileged creatures in the universe and that they possess powers far beyond their dreams;

3) The need for humans to use these powers not just for self-development and self-enhancement but for mutual respect and love;

4) Speaking personally, I'd like to remain in reasonably good shape as long as possible.

Cesar Chavez

Founder and charismatic leader of the United Farm Workers of America, the first farm labor union to organize the Mexican-American migrant farm workers. These days his cause is not merely the rights of farm workers, but their health and the health of consumers he claims are endangered by the use of pesticides on produce. Chavez is as admired and loved in the Mexican-American community as the Rev. Martin Luther King Jr. was among African Americans.

Many years ago I discovered that there is a difference between being of service to people and being a servant. Many people give of their time and resources on behalf of good causes in this world. But so few men or women in our time have had the opportunity to know the true satisfaction that can only come with giving one's life totally in the service of the poor and oppressed. Such is the calling with which those of us in the farm workers' movement have been blessed.

Hans Selye

Endocrinologist and a pioneer of twentieth century medicine (1907-1982); noted for his pathbreaking studies on the body's physiological response to stress. His studies showed that overproduction of adrenal hormones triggered by stress can cause such disturbances as heart disease, arthritis and kidney disease.

Your question about what makes me tick can only be answered by quoting my motto, which is probably the most often cited in connection with the personal code of behavior based on over forty years of stress research:

Fight for the highest attainable aim
But never put up resistance in vain.

This contains the essence of adaptation, since striving for a lofty purpose gives you a margin of security and the satisfaction and accomplishment, while resignation to the inevitable prevents one from squandering one's energy on hopeless causes.

Roger J. Williams

Biochemist and pioneer in the scientific study of vitamins and nutrition (1893-1988); discoverer of pantothenic acid, an important member of the vitamin B family; author of many books, among them You Are Extraordinary *and* Nutrition Against Disease.

In my professional life work, I am essentially an ignorance-fighter. I have no personal enemies; my greatest desire is to dispel ignorance in myself and others. I am not particularly interested in dispelling all kinds of ignorance—ignorance about trivialities I can easily tolerate. I am deeply concerned with the kinds of ignorance we do not dispel in schools—ignorance about individuality in human nature with which we always have to deal, and ignorance about biology and how to take care of our bodies with excellent nutrition and abundant exercise. I would like, before I leave this earthly habitation, to contribute more knowledge and insight into how we, as individuals, can live lives that are physically and mentally healthier. If we can do this, we will inevitably be better adjusted and happier and free from dependence on alcohol and drugs.

Chuck Jones

What Charlie Chaplin and Buster Keaton were to comedy, Chuck Jones is to the animated cartoon. He directed many of the classic Warner Brothers' cartoons featuring Bugs Bunny, Sylvester, Daffy Duck, Porky Pig, Tweetie Bird, Road Runner and Coyote, as well as his own animated specials, such as the award-winning "How the Grinch Stole Christmas."

What doesn't make me tick is a clock, as you can see from the time it took me to answer your letter.

To paraphrase Rimbaud! "Artistry is a cracked kettle upon which we beat tunes for bears to dance to, when all the while we wish to stir the stars to pity."

And yet we must keep beating—"ticking" if you like. Because we are so damned favored to have the opportunity to speak out—even through the voice of a rabbit—or a road-runner.

Garrett Hardin

A persuasive voice for ecological sanity, Garrett Hardin is a biologist, former professor of human ecology and an iconoclastic scientific writer. His influential essay on overpopulation entitled "The Tragedy of the Commons" is one of the most cited scientific papers of the past decade.

I feel that I am the most fortunate of men: more than most, I have, during most of my life, done just about what I want to do—which means that I see myself not so much working as playing.

About 1948 (as I recall) the writings of Benjamin Lee Whorf opened my mind to the mystery of the relations of words to thought. Sensitized to the ubiquitous and almost unceasing self-deception wrought by unexamined words I spend much of my time uncovering other people's taboos and trying to persuade them that they can live without them. (My own taboos? Examining these is beyond *my* power!)

I love the excitement of an argument. I revel in a hostile audience. My life is *fun*.

Albert Szent-Gyorgyi

One of the giants of medical science in the twentieth century (1893-1986).
Hungarian-born biochemist Albert Szent-Gyorgyi discovered Vitamin C
(for which he won the Nobel Prize in 1937); pioneered a radically different way to investigate
and combat cancer; and fathered the whole field of modern muscle physiology.
In addition, Szent-Gyorgyi was a charismatic teacher-researcher and an anti-war activist.

What drives me in the morning to the Lab and keeps me awake at night is that I want to know what cancer is and want to crack this horrid riddle. I am the fourth generation of medical researchers and I must have gotten this from mama.

Timothy Leary

Once a psychology professor at Harvard University, in the 1960s Timothy Leary became
the guru of the psychedelic generation for his advocacy of the use of LSD and other mind-expanding
drugs. For those who feared the consequences of drug use, Leary was viewed as a "corrupter of youth;"
to his followers he was a prophet whose message of "Turn on, tune in, drop out" offered a possible path-
way toward higher consciousness. His adventures with hallucinogenics ultimately brought about
dismissal from Harvard, notoriety and jail. These days Leary travels the lecture circuit and continues to
explore approaches to increase human intelligence.

The Purpose of Life is to discover the Purpose of Life and Live it.

In general this means searching, scoping, scanning continually to decode the genetic algorithms, decipher the memetic codes, the cultural patterns; to map out the stages of human evolution our species is now experiencing, forecast the next waves and to fabricate and communicate memes (ideas) about them in order to encourage and empower individuals to recognize and surf them.

Tactically this means that I spend most of my time learning how to operate my brain, explore my brain, increase the RPM (Realities Per

Minute) efficiency of my brain, i.e. the quantity and quality of signals exchanged.

Professionally I am an Evolutionary Agent. A genetic activist. A performing philosopher.

Specifically this means that I design mutational appliances, intercomsoftware, post-literate linguistic-devices, virtual (electronic) reality programs and use them to communicate with other Evolutionary Agents.

Jacques Barzun

*Jacques Barzun is respected as an eminent historian and critic of culture.
Praised for his vast knowledge of music, painting, literature, philosophy and history,
Barzun is an articulate defender of the humanist tradition.*

Not being a machine, I do not *tick*. What makes me aware of purpose is my mind, all minds being by nature purposive, seeking after ends. (See William James, *Principles of Psychology*). As for the choice of ends in my life, they vary with time, mood, and circumstance, as is true of everybody. Perhaps my prevailing mood and end is that which leads me to try and put some order in the midst of confusion, both internal and external. In the teeth of surrounding chaos I am impelled to act, with as much energy and as little hope as possible, satisfied—whatever the outcome—with the simple assertion: Never-the-less...

Roger Tory Peterson

*Ornithologist and popular bird painter and illustrator, Roger Tory Peterson is the acknowledged
dean of American nature guide editors. His books on birds, beginning with
A Field Guide to The Birds (1934), have revolutionized field identification of birds.*

My orientation toward the natural world is the prime mover of my life. I have become increasingly disturbed by some of the distortions created by technology and am distressed by the problems of over-population in a world where wildlife has less and less space. Therefore I have dedicated my life to informing people about the other living things, "the other nations," with which we share the world. I am basically a teacher, an artist who teaches visually, trying to open the eyes of others.

Edward O. Wilson

Biologist, entomologist, educator and writer. Edward O. Wilson is a leader in the controversial field of sociobiology the emerging scientific discipline whose purpose is to examine the biological bases of behavior. His On Human Nature *won the 1979 Pulitzer Prize in general nonfiction.*

I am a thoroughgoing scientific materialist, which means that mankind makes itself, for itself, with the genetic materials it has assembled over the past five million years or so. The question of surpassing interest therefore is, what are we capable of doing with this remarkable physical inheritance? Twentieth-century man has only begun to find out. The greatest leaps, the farthest perception, and the most complex generalized thought require the assistance of science and technology, yet the personal, human response to these experiences is the province of the arts. The perception of this circumstance, together with the idiosyncracies of my childhood experience, made me a romantic scientist—or perhaps more accurately, a scientific romantic. I perceive of my creative life as the pursuit of a series of difficult, long-range goals that require sustained intense effort. Once attained they allow a brief glimpse of things no one else has seen and thus provide a unique personal measure of what the spirit can do. Witnessing others doing the same thing doesn't give me anything like the same pleasure.

Bud Greenspan

*Master chronicler of the modern Olympics, Bud Greenspan is the acclaimed sports filmmaker of
Sixteen Days of Glory and of the Emmy-award winning 18-part series
"The Olympiad." Greenspan's dramatic documentaries go beyond recording
scenes of winners and losers. His cameras capture the glory of the Olympic games and the
human stories behind the athletes' efforts to reach the top step of the victory platform.*

I have always felt that I was put on this earth to leave something of
myself. It is only in retrospect that I realize the personal satisfaction that
some film I have produced or some piece of personal philosophy can
be used by others to encourage, illuminate, and inspire to give more of
themselves and to fulfill capabilities that for years have remained dormant.

In recent months I have read many reports of senior executives in
the television industry who reply to the criticism of "why is television
so bad" with the words, "If people didn't like it, they wouldn't watch."

This to me is half an answer. I usually reply to that with the words,
"Audiences can feel comfortable with quality as you insist they feel comfortable with mediocrity."

The only real thing I feel special about myself is in the belief that
Emerson was correct. "Speak your thoughts today, for tomorrow others
may speak those same thoughts and the rewards will be theirs," Emerson
wrote.

I think also that talent and creativity have remained constant through
civilization. Creativity, to me, is the process of taking an idea that has
been with us for centuries and producing it with intellect, taste, and sen-
sitivity—talents that can be found in the majority of us with only the
courage to use them distinguishing the few from the many.

I could go on and on, but I think you get my motivation.

Pete Seeger

*Wherever there's been a cause he deemed worth fighting for in America or the world,
Pete Seeger — world traveler, survivor of the House Un-American Activities Committee,
in the forefront of American folk music — has been there singing and helping the cause along.
Whether it's been organizing labor unions in the '40s, fighting for peace or civil rights in the '60s,
or advocating environmental causes in the '80s, Seeger has been there with his banjo and guitar singing
about hammers of justice and bells of freedom and expressing hope for a better world.*

It's unwise to hope that a few glib words can capture the truth, but I'll try.

Hope...that the human race will survive the problems that our cleverness has presented us with. I believe we have a slim (very slim) chance.

Walter Sullivan

*As science editor for the New York Times and author of numerous science-related books, Walter Sullivan
has made such seemingly incomprehensible subjects as theoretical astrophysics or plate tectonics
accessible to thousands of readers.*

My work load and frequent travel make it hard for me to reply to letters, but I have saved yours of a year ago because the question you asked was tantalizing.

After surviving a dozen hair-raising battles in World War II and being spared where friends were not, I came out of the war determined to do what I could to avoid another one. I studied Russian. When I was sent abroad, however, it was to the Far East.

I came to The Times, however, in 1940 eager to help others share my deeply felt musical experiences. I wanted to be a music critic. Today the motivation is somewhat similar. I find the extension of scientific knowledge — of understanding of ourselves and the world around us, out to the farthest limits of observation — a deeply moving aspect of our time. My basic motive is to share this with our readers to the greatest extent possible.

Sidney Hook

Sidney Hook (1902-1989) was considered by many to be America's leading philosopher of pragmatism and democratic pluralism and to others the heir to John Dewey's mantle in the United States. A philosopher for more than forty years at New York University, Hook spoke to the actual conditions of contemporary life.

Answer: The desire to keep the world free from the terrors of totalitarianism.

Arthur Ashe

Arthur Ashe added a new chapter to the history of tennis by becoming the first black male tennis player to win the United States Open (1968) and Wimbledon (1975). In 1979, at age 36, however, he suffered a near-fatal heart attack which forced him to retire from professional tennis. Ashe has proven to be an articulate and effective communicator, writing frequently for newspapers and sports magazines. He is the author of a highly acclaimed autobiography, Off the Court, and the monumental three-volume work entitled A Hard Road to Glory: A History of the African-American Athlete.

It's, for me, very simple — THE PURSUIT OF EXCELLENCE.

John Hope Franklin

John Hope Franklin, professor emeritus of history at Duke University, a teacher and scholar, is considered the "Dean of Black historians." His From Slavery to Freedom (1947), which has won international recognition, is regarded by many as the standard text on African-American history. However, Franklin's scope reaches beyond Black history. Two of his most notable books, The Militant South and A Southern Odyssey, are historical works about white Americans.

112

In reply to your letter I can honestly say that I do not know what makes me "tick." I can say, however, that I work as hard as I do for two reasons. One is to use to the limit all the talents and resources that I possess. Otherwise, I would be profligate and irresponsible. The other is that I have a great desire to put my talents and resources to some constructive purpose — to serve my fellow man.

William V. Shannon

William Shannon (1927-1988) was a journalist for twenty-five years before he was appointed U.S. ambassador to Ireland by President Jimmy Carter in 1977. Previously, he had been Washington correspondent and columnist for the New York Post (1951-1964), and editorial writer fo the the New York Times (1964-1977). Upon returning to the U.S. from Ireland, Shannon joined the faculty of Boston University and wrote for the Boston Globe.

I have thus far pursued three different careers and in each of them had an overriding interest. As a young man I originally wanted to be a historian because I was fascinated by the past. I did not actually become a full-time academic historian but I persisted in my interest and it finally found expression in the writing of my book THE AMERICAN IRISH, published in 1964.

Early on I was deflected from history into commenting on contemporary public affairs. I was in journalism for 27 years and my ambition always was to understand the issues and personalities as well as I could and explain them clearly to readers.

Now I am a diplomat serving as United States Ambassador to Ireland. I would like to help bring peace to this troubled island. The difficulties in Northern Ireland are not an American responsibility and, therefore, anything the United States does there is indirect and supportive in its nature. However, I get personal satisfaction from working toward peace and reconciliation no matter how slowly we make progress toward those objectives.

In the more private sphere of life and human conduct, I am a conservative. I do not believe that radical utopias are possible or that human nature changes except very gradually over centuries of time. I often think over Santayana's lines: "Is your earth happy or your heaven sure? I walk contented to the peopled grave."

Tom Wolfe

Satirist, caricaturist, social critic, novelist, coiner of phrases ("The Me Decade," "Radical Chic"), Tom Wolfe is one the leading chroniclers of American trends. A widely respected reporter, Wolfe came to prominence in the 1960s as a proponent of a style of writing called "New Journalism."

For one as for all in this trough of mortal error: status, maintenance and furtherance thereof.

Pancho Gonzales

The former world champion tennis player was once described as "the most natural tennis player who ever played." In his competitive days Pancho Gonzales was a formidable player who had a rocket-like serve and a fiery temperment. One sports writer described him as "moving over the court like a jungle cat." A more mellow Pancho Gonzales now enjoys semi-retirement and his family.

I suppose what makes me tick is that I enjoy most things around me. I get a big charge out of doing things, watching others do things; watching people fumble and improve. I enjoy when time permits it to try and help when I can.

I don't believe I will ever have the chance to do all the things I would like to do. Therefore, I stay anxiously awaiting day to day with great expectations of what may come. If we were to get into it very deeply to what makes me tick I could probably write a book on it. At present I just don't have the time.

Naturally, all this has to start with good health. Therefore, I wish you good health.

Arun Gandhi

*A verteran journalist and longtime social activist, Arun Gandhi is the grandson of Mahatma Gandhi.
As passionately opposed to discrimination as the elder Gandhi,
Arun Gandhi is currently living in America gathering impressions for a book on racial and
class discrimination as practiced in South Africa, India, and the U.S.*

In the garden of life, human beings ought not be weeds of destruction but flowers and fruits of sustenance and growth. This was an early lesson I learned from my parents and grandparents who also said we are all susceptible to the same weaknesses and pressures as a seedling. To succumb to them is to die either physically or spiritually, but to derive strength from adversity is to grow and radiate goodness. I try, as best I can, to make my sojourn on this earth meaningful and fragrant for all I come in touch with.

Janet G. Travell, **M.D.**

Physician, educator and a pioneer in the study and treatment of musculoskeletal pain and trigger-point therapy. Dr. Janet Travell came to national attention in the 1960s when she became the White House physician to President Kennedy and President Johnson, 1961-1965. She was the first woman ever to hold that post. She is the co-author of the medical text Myofascial Pain and Dysfunction:
The Trigger-Point Manual.

What Makes Me Tick?
The driving force throughout my life has been the desire to help people feel better and enjoy their accomplishments more. When seven years old, I said that I wanted to be a doctor and I never changed my mind. Persistence and curiosity kept me ticking. My physician/magician father built me a foundation of creative thinking from which grew individuality

and self-esteem. I enjoyed complete freedom of choices. Although a pioneer, I never felt lonely.

I never tired of practicing medicine, nor of educating health professionals in new concepts of pain management. My wonderful, supportive husband used to explain how I accomplished so much: "Ask her what she does between midnight and bedtime." In those hours before daybreak, I was reading, thinking, writing — organizing new ideas. Enthusiasm and satisfaction kept me going and still keep me ticking.

THE AUTHOR'S ANSWER TO THE QUESTION

To answer the question, I must go back to the early part of this book, to Robert Louis Stevenson's fable of the monk who heard a bird singing in the woods, and, forgetting his duties, left the monastery and spent the next 50 years of his life searching for and hearing the song of the bird.

I identify with the monk. This fable describes to me what it means to be fully alive — to be involved in an activity so intensely that one loses a sense of time, place, and self, pursuing an object in flight that only you alone can perceive but never can completely catch. That to me defines blessedness.

In my case, however, there are various birds in the woods that I struggle each day to keep my eye on. The first is a sense of curiosity. Like an early explorer burning with a desire to discover a new continent, I seem to be driven by a compulsion, or lust of the mind, to probe and understand the world within and around me. Take away this curiosity and you would deprive me of an important companion and antidote against boredom and disenchantment.

The second bird I seek lives in the theater. There, as an actor on the stage, I find a freedom of expression and communication that can often make me feel like a bird-on-the-wing. In the ideal theater I believe something holy happens: actors put masks on so that those watching can remove their daily masks of fears and worries and rediscover their true and better selves. I also confess I act to get attention.

The third bird I would try to photograph. Whenever I get a chance I like to use a camera and hunt for the esthetic in the face of commonplace things and events, for the flecks of gold shining in the lead. For me, taking pictures is my way of having a deeper conversation with the world.

However, I must be honest. I don't desire to spend all my time in the woods searching. Unlike the monk, I need a home to return to regularly; some safe and secluded place where I can quietely touch down, renew the bonds of affiliation that warm, and not feel desperate. And as time goes on, the bonds become more precious. But, inevitably, I become restless, hear something in the distance, and before I know it am walking towards the sound.

And where will the singing lead me? I don't know the answer to that. The important thing, though, is to follow the sound whereever it may be heard and not be afraid. There's the rub: for it's not just a bird of nature that I seek, it's a whole reason for being — or, if you will, ticking.

Grateful for the opportunity to answer the question,

David Sharpe

YOUR ANSWER TO THE QUESTION

SO, WHAT MAKES YOU TICK?

AFTERWORD

*A*t times during the course of this project I felt like the Little Prince, the interplanetary traveler in Antoine de Saint-Exupéry's story who asked inhabitants of various planets the secret of what is really important in life. In many ways this question—What makes you tick?—is like the Little Prince's query: a child's question, easily asked, but difficult to answer.

To me, however, the question touches a vital existential nerve. It is another way of asking how I should use my time and live my life in a way that will be fulfilling and lasting. Toward what ends am I to struggle? For health, security, pleasure, power, success — the usual goals of a successful life? Or do I seek an early retirement from the business of daily living, planting myself into the ground like a cabbage? Or do I give all to the joy of being, love, and the quest for meaning, the three intangible factors that Will Durant saw as making up the meaning of life? In his story "Prater Violet" author Christopher Isherwood writes:

> There is one question which we seldom ask each other directly; it is too brutal. And yet it is the only question worth asking our fellow travelers. What makes you go on living? Why don't you kill yourself? Why is all this bearable? What makes you bear it?
>
> Would I answer that question about myself? No. Yes. Perhaps...I suppose, vaguely, that it was kind of a balance, a complex of tensions. You did what ever was next on the list. A meal to be eaten. Chapter eleven to be written. The telephone rings. You go off somewhere in a taxi. There is one's job. There are amusements. There are people. There are things to be bought in shops. There is always something new. There has to be. Otherwise, the balance would be upset, the tension would break.

Of course, for many people a major preoccupation of life is basic economic survival and staying ahead of the bill collector. And that's important. However, if there's one thing these letters make clear it is that there's something beyond economic well-being that's critical in how, as Henry Adams said, each person bears his own universe; that there is more to life than just eating and sleeping and that security and comfort are not forever the bottom line of living.

127

So, assuming that health is the first wealth, what keeps a person going? Perhaps, this is what the letters have taught me the most: that the direction to go to find the answer is not forward to look for new continents of thought, but backward to rediscover old ones. In the beginning it was my hope that by learning what makes people tick I would discover some new kind of superconductivity theory of human nature that would benefit mankind, some revolutionary equation for fast, meaningful ticking minus friction and resistance.

But, I'm afraid what defines the movement of electricity under extreme conditions doesn't apply to the problematic currents and challenges of life. Which is why we have to go back—back to renew our encounter with such unscientific conductors as hope and freedom, back to curiosity, imagination, and faith, back to a sense of care, a daring heart and an ideal to strive for. Back to what can't be measured, quantified, or sold in a shopping mall, but is as necessary as oxygen to the blood. Back to what keeps the edifice of civilization and its giant pillars of wealth, power, organization, and culture from becoming an empty citadel. Back to what transcends time and can only be seen with the heart.

These vital intangibles, each with a story to be told, are less for amusement than for our preservation. Like the life-saving tales of the storyteller Scheherazade, who, according to legend, had to tell stories to keep the king from putting her to death, we have to keep revivifying these images with unsleeping effort, or else the light emitted by each image may go out.

Admittedly, "What makes you tick?" isn't an easy question to answer. The business of accounting for one's self is as elusive as stepping on one's shadow. To answer the question fully and faithfully, one would have to write a detailed autobiography. And who has the time? We're all too busy ticking.

AN ALPHABETICAL LISTING
OF CONTRIBUTORS

AN ALPHABETICAL LISTING
OF CONTRIBUTORS

A

B

C

D

E

F

G

H

I

J

K

L

M

N

O

P

S

T

W

Gahan Wilson

Gahan Wilson's cartoons appear regularly in many of today's leading magazines.
Adjectives such as "vile", "morbid", "depraved", "base", "monstrous", "diabolical" and "macabre"
have been all applied to their dark humor. Featuring monsters, aliens, vampires and other grotesque
characters, they are widely popular.

DEAR MR. SHARPE —

IT'S THAT GREAT
BIG KEY SLOWLY TURNING
IN THE MIDDLE OF MY
BACK THAT MAKES ME
TICK — BEST

HI!

Gahan Wilson

C. LILLY ◆ CLAUDE LEVI-STRAUSS ◆ BROOKS ATKINSC
ARLETON S. COON ◆ COLIN WILSON ◆ GEORGES SIME
INUS PAULING ◆ ARTHUR C. CLARKE ◆ COLIN M. TUR
VHEELER ◆ SIR PETER HALL ◆ MADELEINE L'ENGLE ◆ V
ALLACE STEGNER ◆ JAMES J. LYNCH ◆ JOHN PFEIFFER
UDILL ◆ SYBIL LEEK ◆ ARNOLD R. BEISSER ◆ THOR HE\
ES ◆ A. B. GUTHRIE, JR. ◆ ART BUCHWALD ◆ LOWELL 1
IGI BARZINI ◆ GUSTAV ECKSTEIN ◆ RUSSELL BAKER ◆ 1
RT LEKACHMAN ◆ ELROY BODE ◆ H. B. FOX ◆ WILLIA/
EDWARD ABBEY ◆ HENRY STEELE COMMAGER ◆ NIK
RRY GALLOWAY ◆ DEE BROWN ◆ CARLOS MONTOYA
TEALE ◆ ROBERT NISBET ◆ ARCHIBALD MACLEISH ◆ JC
◆ JOHN BOWLE ◆ SIR ALEC GUINESS ◆ WILLIAM MAN
OLLY IVINS ◆ SIR KENNETH M. CLARK ◆ EUGENE KENN
ORTHCOTE PARKINSON ◆ ANDREW M. GREELEY ◆ AR
L ◆ MARY ELLEN MARK ◆ ARCHIBALD COX ◆ MARQU
HOWARD NEMEROV ◆ CHARLES ALAN WRIGHT ◆ A
D JAMES OLMOS ◆ DENTON A. COOLEY ◆ NORMAN
ELYE ◆ CHUCK JONES ◆ ROGER J. WILLIAMS ◆ GARRET
YI ◆ TIMOTHY LEARY ◆ JACQUES BARZUN ◆ ROGER T
VILSON ◆ BUD GREENSPAN ◆ WALTER SULLIVAN ◆ PET
UR ASHE ◆ JOHN HOPE FRANKLIN ◆ WILLIAM V. SH.
NZALES ◆ ARUN GANDHI ◆ JANET G. TRAVELL ◆ WIL
STOPHER FRY ◆ KATHERINE HEPBURN ◆ SIR EDMUN
IKHAIL BARYSHNIKOV ◆ GEORGE SELDES ◆ THOMAS
AALCOLM COWLEY ◆ RAOUL BERGER ◆ RICHARD WIL
AVID L. MILLER ◆ DENIS DE ROUGEMONT ◆ ERMA BC
M CLANCY ◆ BOB KANE ◆ JOHN CALLAHAN ◆ HAZEL
HN HENRY FAULK ◆ DAME JOAN SUTHERLAND ◆ JOH
◆ BROOKS ATKINSON ◆ GEORGE GAYLORD SIMPSON
ON ◆ GEORGES SIMENON ◆ HARRISON SALISBURY ◆ L
ARKE ◆ COLIN M. TURNBULL ◆ JOHN ARCHIBALD W
LEINE L'ENGLE ◆ VINCENT PRICE ◆ JANE GOODALL ◆ V
H ◆ JOHN PFEIFFER ◆ PATRICK MOORE ◆ HARRY M. C
ISSER ◆ THOR HEYERDAHL ◆ RICHARD NELSON BOL
ALD ◆ LOWELL THOMAS ◆ CHARLES OSGOOD ◆ LUIG
ISSELL BAKER ◆ THEODOR S. GEISEL (DR. SEUSS) ◆ ROB
H. B. FOX ◆ WILLIAM BURROUGHS ◆ MORTON MIN
COMMAGER ◆ NIKKI GIOVANNI ◆ TERRY GILLIAM ◆
CARLOS MONTOYA ◆ ANTONIA BRICO ◆ EDWIN WA
HIBALD MACLEISH ◆ JOHN CIARDI ◆ BRAND BLANSH

SO
WHAT MAKES
YOU TICK?

"HUMAN BEINGS LIVE ON MEANING; we demand purpose.... With this in mind, my question to you is: What makes *you* tick? You are a person whose work and intelligence I admire. What makes you tick? Would you let me use your answer in my book?"

David Sharpe wrote this letter to over a hundred notable people, including George Burns, Cesar Chavez, Katherine Hepburn, Mikhail Barishnikov, Claude Levi-Strauss, Isaac Asimov, Jane Goodall, Dr. Seuss, William S. Burroughs, Carlos Montoya, and Gahan Wilson. You will be fascinated by their answers when you read **SO, WHAT MAKES YOU TICK?**

TEN SPEED PRESS

$8.95

ISBN 0-89815-372-7

50895>

9 780898 153729